MIND

the

Movement

By Anil Jain

ACKNOWLEDGEMENT

My gratitude to all the wise people around and the great wealth of religious scriptures that helped me learn how to inquire and investigate on the origin of movements and source of all actions.

Table of Contents

What is a movement?..1

Observing Movement...15

Realm of Knowledge 47

Nature of Truth 61

Observation and Action are One..77

What movements are observed? 95

Observation with Memory...135

Present Moment is the key 155

Mind, the Player..175

Memory, Known & the Backdrop...207

Nature of the Mind..232

Wrapping it all...254

1

What is a movement?

Neera is introduced to fine details of observing and identifying a movement

It was evening already and I left office to reach my home after a five minute drive. My daughter, Neera came running to me, looking excited. I asked, "So, did you get your driving license?" She nodded. It had been almost three years since she had been having a learner's permit and was driving with us learning slowly but consistently. Before handing over a responsibility of driving to our youngster, we wanted to be fully confident that she was ready to handle all kinds of situations that she might face on road. It had been a long journey for her, and she had shown her frustration many times as all of her friends were already driving their cars to school.

She asked me, "Papa, why do we all have to go through all the training before driving?"

I said, "It is so that everybody driving on the road follows the same set of rules. This allows for a balanced, harmonious movement among everybody and ensures the least accidents and disruptions on the roads."

She asked again, "Why do we have to be trained and controlled through rules and regulations? Are not humans the most intelligent of all species?"

I said, "Yes, this is what we think".

She got surprised, "Why? Do you have any doubts about it?"

I said, "It all depends on what do we mean by being intelligent. If you look around, the whole universe is moving. Every kind of creature lives on the planet, and they all seem to move quite comfortably among their colonies. Have you ever wondered if they all are taught some rules before they start moving among their territories? If the ants, flies, mosquitos, termites and birds have never attended any training program, how do they all move in huge numbers, without crashing into each other?"

She looked curious, "I suppose not. Last weekend when I was in the Desert Breeze Park, a small kid threw a pebble among a group of pigeons; and all of them instantly flew away. I didn't see a single one confused, tripping over or hitting another pigeon. And do you remember the huge aquarium that we saw on our trip to West Coast last summer?

Even though there are hundreds of different kinds of fishes that continue to swim in that enclosure all the time, I don't think I ever saw any issue with coordination among them. They seem to be moving almost ignorant of other fishes and yet getting hit or smashed by another one is out of question."

I smiled. I asked, "And what about humans who are not driving, just being on their foot, in a busy place?"

She got energized. She exclaimed, "Oh! You won't believe it. As soon as a panic is caused, everybody starts running all over, totally confused. Some of them get tripped and fall. Others keep on running wildly while crushing others who have fallen. You must see how many people get killed every time there is a stampede caused by sudden fear!"

I agreed quietly. I thought that it was an end of our discussion, so walked towards the couch and got seated on one side.

Neera came and sat by my side.

"So, what do you think?" She asked.

"About what?" I lazily asked back.

"About the movement." She said.

"What movement?" I tried to sound ignorant even though I knew she wanted to explore more. I wanted to see how much interest she had in order to know how far to stretch this topic.

"..about the movement that goes on in the whole universe. Who governs it, controls it? Who decides how a creature will behave among all other creatures, of its own community, or of other communities?" She came with a big question, which I had not expected.

"I think there must be some rule which governs all movements." I said.

"Is the rule different for birds, ants, flies, fishes, cattle and humans?" She asked.

"I believe that the rules must be same for everything." I said.

"Why so?" She asked.

"It is because that keeps the things simple." I said.

"Why would the things be needed to be simple?" She asked

"The universe consists of all varieties of creatures of varying complexities and body structures. Some are single celled, and some have only a few kinds of senses. It would not make sense if there were complicated sets of rules that were not understood or known by creatures having less developed system of interpreting. The rules have to be so simple that every little piece of life knows it. Since the universe seems to be doing a pretty good job for almost an eternity, it must be so." I said.

"What are those rules?" She asked.

"What rules?" I wanted to be sure what she was up to.

"The rules which govern the movement of everything in this universe. The rules that are so simple that an ant knows, a bird knows, a single celled bacterium knows but the humans don't seem to know." She said.

"Are you sure you want to go into this?" I checked. I didn't want to go half way only to find that she wasn't much interested.

"Yes, Papa. I do. Please tell me about the whole movement that is going around us." She said with conviction.

I was not sure if I would be able to tell anything that might satisfy her, but I knew that we had at least picked up an idea worth exploration. I saw my wife approaching with a cup of hot tea. I held the cup in my hand, got comfortable on the couch, and started to think where to start from.

"What is a movement?" I asked her, carefully taking a sip from the cup.

She seemed to think for a moment trying to arrange words into what might make sense. Then she answered, "A movement is when something goes from here to there. How else can you describe it?"

I asked her to get one of the hardbound dictionaries from my bedroom shelf. She didn't move. Instead, she picked up her phone and tapped a few times. "You know, what the dictionary.com says about this?" she asked.

I waited for her to say. She showed her phone to me instead. The page showed the following definition of the word - *movement*.

> movement
>
> noun
>
> 1. the act, process, or result of moving
> 2. a particular manner or style of moving

Before I could say that the definition didn't help much, she was already up to finding out what does the dictionary.com say about the word 'moving', the clue that the description contained. The page showed the following meanings for the word - *moving*.

> moving
>
> adjective
>
> 1. capable of or having movement.
> 2. causing or producing motion.

At this point, I wondered if there was someone who really checked to see if these dictionaries served any purpose. They definitely did not provide an answer. All they did was to repeat the question in a different way. Maybe that is the best a dictionary could do; describe a given word or a problem in such a variety of ways that some clue may help you move on. Not losing hope, I saw that it gave another unique clue and asked her to check if it describes the word 'motion' in any other way. At last, there was some clarity about the word, which was described like this.

> motion
>
> noun
>
> 1. the action or process of moving or of changing place or position; movement
> 2. power of movement

According to the online dictionary, a movement is some kind of action or process of changing place or position. This was as good a description of the word as we would have expected. I looked at Neera, and she looked back with a surprise on her face. "What!" She said. "I already know that. How can knowing a definition help me with knowing anything about it? It is just explaining the word by means of some more words while I am still clueless."

She saw me smiling. I guess she figured out what happened just now. It had happened in the past too; whenever she accidentally discovered something totally new accidentally, I gave her the same smile. She repeated again, this time slowly. "How can knowing a definition help me know anything about a thing!"

> **"How can knowing a definition help me know anything about a thing!"**

We had started our discussion wondering about the whole movement around us, the movement called, the universe. We wanted to explore if there was a very simple rule that each and every bit of the universe was aware of and was following it very precisely. In the process, she figured out that providing a definition or a description of any word does not give you any more knowledge about it. A dictionary can only provide another set of words for a word. *If you would look for a 'question', you would only get a 'problem', not an 'answer' in a dictionary.*

We figured out that if we wanted to know something totally new about something, we could not depend on the existing knowledge, which is what a definition does. Moreover, if the definition of something is totally in terms of something we do not know, any explanation it provides will be useless. For example, someone who does not know anything about the French language will not find French to French dictionary useful. This is what we were going through currently. We wanted to explore on some unknown aspects of the 'movement', and had chosen to refer to a dictionary, not knowing that it will end up giving a general description of the word but otherwise be useless for the purpose of gaining some insight.

I sat quietly for a couple of minutes. I kept staring blankly in front of myself not really looking at something. Suddenly my attention went to the side table. I noticed there was a spider moving on the side of the vase lying on the table. I thought for a minute and then asked Neera.

"Do you see that vase? Is it moving?"

"No" she said.

"And do you see the spider on the vase. Is that moving?"

She looked at it for a moment and noticed it crawling slowly and steadily, trying to reach up to the top of the vase. "Yes, it is moving to the top." She said.

"So you know that the vase is not moving. And you also know that the spider is moving." I said.

"Yes, it is not some rocket science. I have known this always." She said.

Even though she had mentioned another one of those discoveries that would have made me give a mysterious smile, I resisted the temptation. I didn't want to digress from the topic we were on and start on the topic of inherent intelligence that each and every living being is born with. The intelligence that governs the whole universe, one that allows one to 'know', to be aware, to sense and to make movements, that drives everything, in a harmony; the knowledge that has already been with all of us, all the time. The knowledge that we were trying to remember through the very discussion we were trying to have. No doubt, she had known many things already without someone formally teaching her.

I asked her instead, "Can you try to figure out what differentiates a movement from non-movement. What are the necessary conditions which, when present, one can 'know' that a movement exists? She said that the vase continued to remain on the table, whereas the spider changed position on the vase. I asked her to slowly repeat what she said and write down what seemed like important points. She took out her notebook and made a table.

Non-Movement	Movement
Vase	Spider
Table	Vase
No change in position	*Changed Position*

I was impressed by her ability to pay attention to the little details. I asked her if she thought of anything else that seemed important. She didn't think so.

"Do you think the vase will always remain stationary? Or do you think the spider will always be moving?" I asked.

"Obviously not", she said. "It is possible that we might remove the vase sometime in the future for the purpose of cleaning, or replacing it." The spider will also not always be doing what it is doing right now. It might want to rest sometime, or may sit still wait for its prey to get caught in its web."

"So can you say that it is a matter of time when something may be in motion?" I asked.

"Yes, it has to be. Nothing ever remains the same." She said.

"And is it possible to know about any movement instantly?" I asked her.

"You mean to say if I could tell if the spider was moving the moment you asked me?" she wanted to confirm what exactly I wanted to know.

"Yes. Immediately; the moment you saw the spider."

"No, it's not possible. A thing cannot be at two places at the same time. In order to see if it changed position, there has to be a period of time, however small it might be." She replied confidently.

"You are right! Since a thing cannot occupy two different places or positions at the same time, a movement cannot exist on any given instant.

Movement happens in time. There has to be a finite period of time during which a movement can be observed.

Movement happens in time. There has to be a finite period of time during which a movement can be observed. Do you want to make changes to what you wrote about the essential things for a movement to happen?" I asked her.

"It sure makes sense!" She said. "You mean to say that the change in time becomes the fourth necessary element for a movement." She quickly added another item to her table, which looked like this.

Non-Movement	Movement
Vase	Spider
Table	Vase
No change in position	*Changed Position*
Change in Time	Change in Time

"Now that we have listed out what might constitute a movement or a non-movement in this case, would you like to generalize it?" I asked her.

"I am not sure why do we want to do that?" She asked.

"Remember, we want to explore the universe with its various movements going around? In order to understand what a movement is, we should be able to create a template, and use it every time we want to observe the universe for its various movements, subtle or strong, visible or invisible, destructive or creative, painful or pleasurable." I tried to bring her attention back to her original question, the great puzzle that the universe is.

"I don't believe we could generalize something to such an extent that could cover every possible thing in this world!" she said.

"Well, the best way is to try and figure this out as we go". I said.

"But, I am not good at looking at the world in general terms. I am good at focusing precisely at some limited area. I can never visualize how things fit in bigger picture." She said.

"Let me try to help you." I offered, "But not so soon." I saw that Nilu, my wife had finished her tea and was sitting quietly hearing our discussion. "Why don't we continue our discussion tomorrow evening? This way you can go and do your studies while I will try to gather some thoughts."

As she started to gather her books, she suddenly stopped and started scribbling something in her notebook. I could guess that she would have found a piece worth remembering from our discussion. I peeked and found this is what she had noted down.

RULE 1: Movement happens in time.

She gathered her books and went to her room. I looked at Nilu and smiled. I asked her if she got bored with our discussion. She said anything was better than watching some dumb television show in the name of relaxation. We sat there for another fifteen minutes and then she left for the kitchen to take care of the dinner. I too got up to change and settle in the silence of the bedroom for the nightly meditation.

As I sat down in the silent darkness of the room, the voices started becoming clear. The occasional sound of vessels from the kitchen, the sound of strings of Ukulele from Neera's room, and the starting and shutting of the air-conditioner continued to fill the silence. The thoughts continued to fill the occasional gaps between the sounds, how we had spent those years making our daughter practice the driving, how the current traffic has become more and more busy and drivers unpredictable, how important it is to be attentive while driving. Then suddenly I became aware of the thoughts going through my mind. The movement of the thoughts came to a halt as soon as I became aware of them. The sounds were still there, the sounds of strings, vessels and of the air-conditioner. The movement was all it was about, either the presence of it, or the absence of it. I wonder, if there was anything anytime other than a movement, the movement called the universe, the movement called the thoughts, the movement called the mind. Soon I lost track of the thoughts and also of the time. I don't know how long it took for me to open the eyes, but when I looked at the clock, I found that I had been sitting for about fifty minutes. I remembered what my daughter had noted in her notebook. Movement happens in time. To say it differently, when there is no movement, there is no time. When the movement of the thoughts (might have) stopped, the sense of the time stopped too.

2

Observing Movement

Neera finds out about the frame of reference, the observer, and the relative nature of observation

I did not get a chance to talk to Neera again for a few days. She became busy with her studies and was mostly locked in her room. It was Saturday afternoon and I was sitting in the patio. For the month of May, it was a cool sunny day. The sky was clear and a few birds were in sight. I might have been there for about ten or fifteen minutes, that I saw Neera coming out of the sliding the patio door. She said, "I have been watching you from inside. You don't seem to be too busy. I thought it would be a right time to pick up our discussion from where we left".

I asked her if she was done with her exams. She said her term exams had finished, and she had finished with her routine studies and homework for the week. She asked, "Have you thought of a general description of a movement?"

I said, "I didn't give any thought to it since we last left the discussion. But that should not stop us from investigating about it, if that is what we want to do right now."

She asked, "Isn't this a perfect time to continue?"

I agreed. No time is a bad time when it comes to enquiring and finding out the unknown.

I asked her to show her notebook where she had noted down the four essential things that were required in order to figure out if a movement existed. The table showed two distinct cases.

Case 1 (No Movement)	Case 2 (Movement)
Vase Table *No change in position* Change in Time	Spider Vase *Changed Position* Change in Time

In the first case, there were two things, the vase and the table. The vase did not seem to change position over a period of observed time. In the second case there were two things, the spider and the vase. The spider was seen to change position over a period of observed time. There are two things in both cases. One thing is observed to move or not move from the point of view of the other thing. The fixed entity seems to provide a point of reference with respect to which the change in position is observed for the other entity.

I thought of the following definition, and asked Neera to write it in her book.

> A movement happens when all of the following are present
> - An entity, and
> - Another entity (working as a frame of reference), and
> - Change in Space (position, location), and
> - Change in Time

She quietly spent some time looking at it. She asked, "I am not sure what do you mean by a frame of reference".

I told her that a frame of reference or a point of view is the way something is observed. Things are seen differently based on how they are looked. There is a lot of conflict in the world between people of various cultures, countries, race and religion. It is all because they have their own unique way of looking at things and interpreting it in their own way.

Then I asked her, "Do you know if the sun goes around the earth?"

She said, "No. We all have studied in science that it is the earth that moves around the sun. The rotation of the earth around its axis gives an impression that the sun rises in the east and sets in the west".

I asked her, "But from the point of view of the earth, does the sun not seem to rise every morning in the east?"

She said, "Yes, this is how it seems".

I asked her again, "And is it not true that from the earth, the sun seems to travel all day from east to west, and finally sets in the west in the evening?"

She said, "Yes, this is how it seems too".

I said, "The movement of the sun is a movement seen from the point of view of the earth. In the same way, the movement of the spider was seen from the point of view of the vase. The earth or the vase provides the frame of reference or the point of observation".

She asked, "What do you mean by observation?"

I asked her back, "What do you think an observation is?"

She said, "To observe means to see or to watch."

I asked "What does the dictionary say?"

She referred to the dictionary page on her phone and showed me the long list of interpretations that the word 'observe' could have. It looked like this.

observe

verb
- to see, watch, perceive, or notice.
- to regard with attention
- ..

I said, "You are quite right; Most of the time we do observe through our eyes. But observation does not mean just seeing. It means noticing, perceiving or simply paying attention."

I wanted to probe her more on this subject, so I asked her, "Tell me, how someone perceives?"

> **Observation does not mean just seeing. It means noticing, perceiving or simply paying attention.**

She replied, "We perceive through our sense organs. We can see, hear, touch, taste and smell. And I recently read somewhere that we just don't perceive through our five senses. We also have a sense of balance, temperature, and the ability to know spatial location of our body parts, known as proprioception."

I was surprised, "That's wonderful! Even I didn't think that our sense of balance, or the ability to locate our own body parts could be one of the senses that we could not classify under any of the known five senses!"

I continued with my exploration and asked, "So what do you think observing is?"

She looked excited. She said, "So we observe by means of our ability to perceive or sense, which could be any of the sense mechanism of our body.

I asked her, "Could we say that to observe is to know?"

She thought for some time. She said, "Probably."

I said, "We tend to perceive or sense using our sense organs in order to know. Or we could say that we know through perceiving. When we touch a hot surface, we sense heat, and therefore 'know' that the surface is hot. When we hear a sound, we sense it through our hearing, and we know that there must be something that might have made the sound."

I continued, "In short, can we not say that to observe is to know?"

She agreed. And what followed was obvious. She promptly noted this in her notebook.

RULE 2: To Observe is to Know.

She asked, "You said that the point of view is always needed for a movement. Is that true?"

I said, "Yes, if all four requirements are met then a movement exists. What moves depends on who is observer or the point of reference. The point of view or the frame of reference is the non-moving ground of observation. In absence of any point of reference or an observer there is no movement".

She said, "Papa, can you please slow down? I am not sure if I could understand anything. You said so many things at once. You seem to be using the words such as point of view, point of observation, frame of reference and observe interchangeably as if they all mean the same thing."

I said, "I do. They all mean the same thing."

She was confused, "But how can the frame of reference be the observer? In our first example, the table was the frame of reference, and in the second case it was the vase. How can we call the vase or the table as observers?"

I was glad that she was paying attention. Sooner or later I wanted to bring in the concept of the Observer, the Observed and the Observation. It seemed to be the correct time to introduce the Observer.

I asked her, "Imagine that in the second case, it was you instead of the vase. Let's assume that you are not too afraid of spiders, and that you observed one moving on you."

She said, "But I am afraid of spiders. Can we use something else in place of a spider?"

I said, "OK. What about an ant on your hands?"

She said, "An ant is no better than a spider. But I think I will manage with an ant for now."

I said, "You notice the movement of an ant on your body either as a crawling sensation or as a relative change in its position as seen through eyes. What are the two entities involved in the movement according to our originally defined criteria?

She said, "Well, the first entity is the ant and the second one as frame of reference is my body".

I asked, "And what is the movement observed against?

She replied, "The movement of the ant is observed against my body."

I asked, "So, can we not say that the movement of the ant is being observed against the body, or simply, being observed by the body?"

She said, "I suppose we can. But it looks fine in case of a living person. How can we call a vase an observer?"

I asked, "If you were to put a set of eyes, nose and ears on the vase and write a fictional comic strip about the vase and the spider, would any of your readers have any problem saying that the vase is an observer?"

She seemed happy. She had been finding difficulty in considering a non-living thing being called as an observer. But it became clear to her that a frame of reference was simply being called an observer, because it was functioning as the point of observation.

> **It became clear to her that a frame of reference was simply being called an observer, because it was functioning as the point of observation.**

She said, "Oh, I get it! The earth is so huge and we humans can observe the movement of the sun, moon and other asteroids in relation to the earth, from the point of view of the earth. In that sense we are like the eyes and ears of the earth."

I said, "True. Imagine some aliens watching from a distance and talking among themselves that the earth has seen our movement!"

She said, "The more I think about this, the more it makes sense. If I think of the vase as a huge structure like our earth, and if there are thousands of little organisms living on its surface, they would observe the movement of the spider from the reference of the vase. In all practical sense, it would not be different than saying that the vase has noticed the movement of spider."

I saw Neera pick her artfully decorated notebook and starting to record something. She wrote

RULE 3: Frame of reference (of a movement) is the point of observation, or simply the Observer.

Neera looked confused. She said, "I think you said so many things at a time. I am not sure if I understand everything. I can believe that all movements can be observed from the point of view of a reference point. But you also said that if something was not observed, then it didn't happen for the observer. I don't believe this. If I don't go to class tomorrow, will the teacher not teach the class? If I sleep all day, will the sun not rise or set? I am also not sure why would the point of observation have to be a fixed point. Why can't both the observer and observed be moving?"

I said, "I can see that it is too much to grasp. Let's go on this slowly, one by one."

Then I repeated what she told me, telling her, "You said that you understand all movements are observed from the point of view of a reference. Let's call it the point of observation, or simply the observer. You are not sure why the observer is non-moving. Is that right?"

"Yes." She said.

"Let's play a game." I asked, "Can you get me some sheets of papers and make small rectangular pieces, about 4-6 inches big?" I remembered something from my primary school experiment that our teacher had shown once.

She made a few square pieces. Then I asked her to make two holes big enough to put her fingers in them. She got ready with the papers in a few minutes. They were pieces like this.

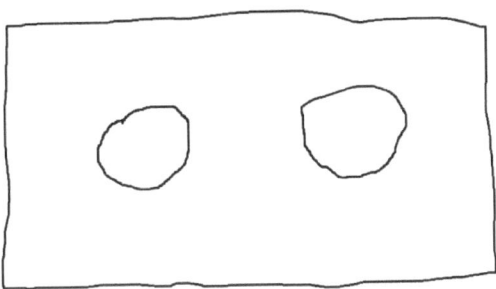

I asked her if she would try to put a finger in each of the holes and try to rip both the holes by pulling apart. She said "That should be easy!" and thought of giving it a try. She picked a paper and put a finger of each hand in the holes.

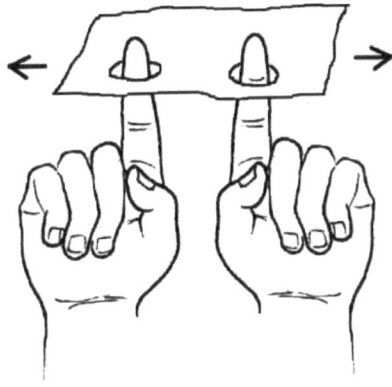

She pulled her fingers to the side and expected to see both the holes be torn together. However, she was surprised that one hole was intact. She was able to tear the paper through one hole only.

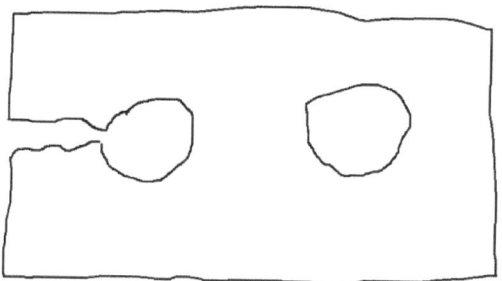

She wanted to try again. She picked another paper and saw that she could tear only one hole. She continued trying till she finished all the papers. Each time, her attempt to pull through both the holes in paper resulted in only one hole being torn.

I asked, "Do you see what's happening here?"

She said, "Only one gets torn!"

I asked, "Are you not trying to move through the holes such that each experiences a movement relative to other?"

She nodded.

I continued, "And when two forces are at action, the weaker of the two starts getting torn while the strong becomes the point of reference; the point of reference, that does not move. In no case will both holes experience the movement (tearing up), *a motion is always relative*, one of the two has to be the fixed point of reference for the other movement.

She said, "It is an interesting experiment. I will be glad to show it to my friends someday.

However, I am not too sure I understand that one of the two things which we call as the frame of reference has to be fixed or non-moving."

I said, "Let me give you a scenario. Imagine a vast ocean with nothing else but water in sight. There are no clouds in the sky, no birds or no mountains, but just water everywhere. You are alone in your boat. Is there a way to figure out if your boat is still or moving?"

Picture: 2.1 Each boat observes the other with reference to itself

She said, "I see, it is impossible to figure out if the boat is moving. Even if I can sense the engine vibrations in the boat, its possible that the engine might be running and the boat might not be moving."

I said, "Let's imagine another boat in sight. If you see the other boat going away from you, then you are observing the movement of the other boat from the fixed position of your boat. The only estimate you can make about the speed of the other boat is how fast it is moving towards you or moving away from you. For example, you might say that the other boat is moving at the speed of 500 meters per minute away from your boat. Your boat might be actually moving in the ocean at a speed of 4000 meters per minute, but in your observation, the speed relative to the ocean does not exist. You observe the movement of the other boat from a non-moving position"

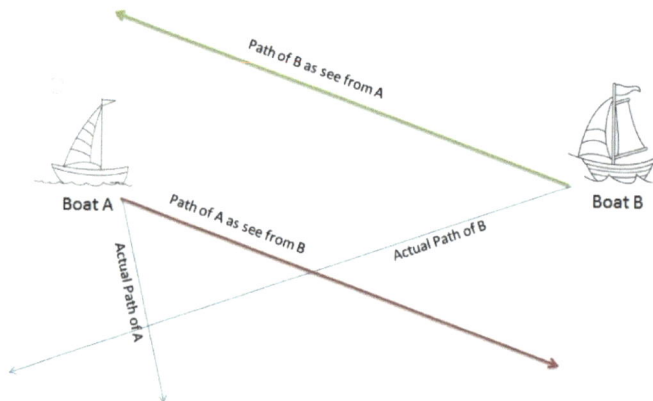

Picture: 2.2 The actual and relative movement as seen from each boat

I asked Neera if she still had doubts how could the frame of reference (of observation) be called non-moving when the observation could happen from a moving entity. She replied, "I understand that the thing observing could possibly be moving in physical sense, but for all practical purposes, the movement in the observed thing is seen with respect to a fixed non-moving reference. Just like when we drive on a freeway at a speed of 60 miles per hour along with all the other traffic going at the same pace, we do not see any perceivable movement among the cars. They seem pretty stationary."

"You made a correct observation", I said.

"And also in a moving train, when we drop something, it falls straight down. Even though we might be moving at a great speed with the train, we do not observe any strange behavior in the path of the dropped thing. While inside the moving train, everything moves with us such that we there is no relative motion among us." She continued.

I nodded. "Have you considered that fact that if the observations were in-fact possible to be made from moving frame, then it wouldn't have been possible to record those observations and watch them again from a fixed position like we watch all recorded or live events on a fixed screen of a television or a projector sitting firmly in our couches." I said.

Neera said, "This never occurred to me!" Then added, "And as we are talking, the earth (along with us) is not only rotating on its axis, it is also moving at a great speed around the sun. But we do not experience this reality in our daily life and take the earth's surface as the fixed non-moving ground of all activity." She added her last bit of knowledge. Then she went on the note this piece of information in her notebook.

RULE 4: Frame of reference or Observer is non-moving.

Seeing her writing in the book, I got an idea. There are two kinds of people, those who use words to explain or understand, and those who use pictures to explain or understand. While Neera was the first kind, I was of the second kind, one who understood in pictures. Pictures have no language; they can be understood by someone who doesn't know your language.

Pictures can be used to build a bigger idea based on the smaller ideas, just like a picture of a wall can be made by combining a lot of smaller pictures of bricks. I thought of introducing Neera to the world of pictures in order to understand complex ideas. I showed this picture to Neera. It is called a comparator which has two inputs and one output. The output is simply the difference of the two inputs.

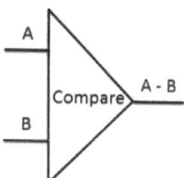

Picture: 2.3 A symbol of a comparator

I asked Neera if she could use the understanding of the observation of movement and try to explain using the model of a comparator. She looked at the picture of the comparator and figured out that the two inputs to the comparator were like the observation of two different objects in an observation. The process of comparison was like observation involving change in space and time. She drew the following model of the observation in her notebook.

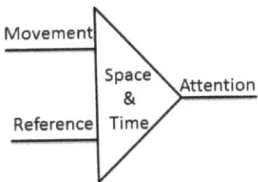

Picture: 2.4 Observation of a movement

I saw that Neera was quiet, busy in some thought. After some time, she closed her notebook and asked me, "We have been talking about observing the movement of things, but what about the things that don't move? Don't we observe things even if they are not moving?"

I said, "Observation (of movement) exists as long the four points are satisfied in the condition that we laid down in the beginning."

She didn't seem convinced, "Where's a change in place in case of a non-moving object? Don't we observe them?"

I said, "Good question! You tell me how something gets recognized as an object."

She replied, "There is knowledge of an object when it can be seen, touched or felt through our senses".

I asked, "When does someone feel a touch, or a taste? When is it that one senses something?"

She was not sure. She said, "I don't know what you would want me to say."

I said, "Let me help you with that. Don't you feel something touching, when just a moment before the sense of touch, there was no sense of touch? You wear your eyeglasses all day. You wear your shoes all the time when you go out. Do you feel the touch of your glasses or shoes all the time?"

She said, "Oh, I see! We feel the touch of things only at the time they come into contact with us initially."

I said, "This is same with all senses whether seeing, hearing, touching, tasting or smelling. We can sense the change in sensation but not the continuous sensation."

She said, "You mean only changes are noticed! If there is no change, there is no noticing?"

I said, "There is a television set on the table. You observe the TV set at the time of transition from watching no TV set to watching the TV set on the table. Once the object has been noticed, and there is no more movement in the object, the observation ceases".

Neera said, "I have never heard anything like this before! It is so strange. You mean we never notice something if there is no change?"

I said, "It is what noticing or learning means. What is there to learn about something that does not change once you have known it? Assume there is a blank wall in front of you. You observe it completely – its colors, its touch, its roughness. Once you have known it so completely that there is nothing else to know, what do you do? You never notice the wall! All you notice later is any change associated with the wall, such as a new hole, a new color, a creeping insect or a new crack."

Neera said, "It is interesting. I never thought about that. Can we talk about this more? I would not like to make something a rule unless I completely see the truth about it."

I said, "Let's talk about this."

Then I continued on the investigation, "We start gathering knowledge or start learning based on our senses; Right?"

Neera said, "That's right. Senses are the primary origin of all our learning and knowing."

I asked, "Do you know that all sensory knowing is relative?"

Neera said, "I am not sure what it means."

I said, "Let's take a few examples. When you touch something, when do you say it is hot or cold?"

Neera said, "When its temperature is higher than my skin, I say it's hot. When its temperature is lower than my skin temperature, I say it's cold."

I said, "Your skin temperature is around 37 °C. If you come in contact with an object which is at a temperature of 10 °C, you can sense it as cold. When you hold it in one hand and hold another object at 0 °C, you can see that this object is cooler than the other."

Neera said, "Yes. I can feel the coolness in relation to my own skin temperature."

I said, "And the same applies to warm and hot objects too. You can always tell if an object is warm because it means that its temperature is higher than your skin."

Neera said, "Yes, this is right."

I said, "This means that the sensing organ, the skin, behaves like a background on which the sensations of temperature are noticed as long it is different than the background. This means that all that is noticed on this background is the change, or the relative temperature."

Neera nodded.

I asked her, "What does the skin notice about an object's temperature which is also at 37 °C. If you touch this wood floor, what do you feel?"

Neera said, "It's neither hot nor cold."

I said, "This means the knowledge about temperature doesn't exist for you."

Neera said, "I hope that's what it means."

I said, "Does it not mean that not only is only a change noticed in presence of a background, or a frame of reference, but the noticing completely ends once the change ends?"

Neera nodded in agreement.

I asked her, "Though you don't notice the temperature of the floor, does the floor not have some temperature?"

Neera said, "It does have a temperature of about 37 degrees. But I don't notice it because it is the same as my body."

I said, "The observation of temperature from the frame of reference (skin temperature) is not possible if it is the same as the frame of reference. What does it say?"

Neera responded, "Observer cannot see itself?"

I was impressed. How else could it be said? *An observer cannot see itself.* A skin cannot sense its own temperature.

Everything that has the temperature of the skin cannot be sensed in terms of its temperature. In the same way as an eye can see everything but not itself. How could a knife cut itself or a fire burn itself? I told Neera, "Have you not noticed sometimes looking for your glasses unaware that you are already wearing them? Does a mad person ever know about his madness? If you are angry, do you know at the moment that you are angry? If you forgot something, do you know at that moment that you are forgetting? An observer can see everything that it is not. *Anything seen, heard or felt cannot be the part of the observer ever.*"

Neera made a nothing in her book. She was well aware that even though she was writing that an observer cannot see itself, she was using the word *seeing* for *knowing*.

RULE 5: Observer cannot see itself.

Neera said, "Let's talk more about this. Isn't this surprising that when we start pondering over any issue in depth, we seem to come up with something totally new! We were talking about the nature of knowledge, and we not only figured out about the quality of observation always being relative but also about the unique quality of observing; that the observer can never ever be seen or known."

I said, "Let's take another example of our senses. How do we know about the size of anything?"

Neera said, "We know about the size by measuring it."

I asked, "What is a measurement?"

Neera said, "Measuring is a comparison, with some other already known thing."

I said, "So you mean to say that knowing about a size of an object is through comparison with some other object. There is no absolute knowledge about the size, but only if it is bigger or smaller than other thing. Just like knowing the temperature of an object!"

Neera said, "Yes, it seems there is no absolute size of anything. When I am among the kids, I am the biggest. But when I am among my own classmates, I am the smallest. There is no absolute knowledge called a standard size; it's always in relation to some other object."

I asked, "Can you think of any other knowledge that you could think as absolute?"

Neera said, "We study history in our class. Is that not absolute knowledge?"

I said, "What do you study in history? Isn't it about recording of some facts observed from some point of reference? Didn't we say that any observation *seen* from a frame of reference is relative change as perceived from the point of view of the reference? When a slave country records its history as freedom fight, the ruling country records it as an act of revolt, violence, and lawlessness by its colony."

Neera asked, "What about geography? The countries, landscapes, trees and nature; are they not absolute knowledge?"

I asked, "They all are observed through your senses such as eyes, ears, and nose to give an impression about the beautiful landscape, wonderful fragrances and mysterious sounds. Does the nature exist in the same way to someone blind, someone deaf, someone mute? Isn't it relative to how one perceives? What seems beautiful to you might be seen as not so beautiful by other. What is night to you and is a time to relax, is not the same to an owl or a bat or many insects. The geography as known by you is completely different than the geography known by another living creature such as a fish, bird or an ant."

Neera said, "It seems I never thought any of this in detail. When we look at it this way that all entry points for knowledge and learning are the senses, then there is no denying that there can never be an absolute learning or knowledge about anything in this universe (through senses)."

I could see that Neera was overwhelmed with such an immense fact. We don't notice something already known? We can't notice something already known? Do we always have to depend on something to change in order to notice? Aren't we all going to go on collecting all the relative and incremental changes as knowledge while becoming a huge bag of old memories of stale facts of everything around us? If a change is all we can notice, can we never know completely about anything? Is that the ultimate truth? It was something huge! Neera was sitting silent trying to digest this new piece of knowledge. I could see her writing in her notebook.

RULE 6: Only Change is Noticed.

I remembered that Neera had a doubt about observing non-moving objects. We had said that we can only observe a movement, when there is a relative change in place and time between two objects, one of them being the frame of reference. We also called such observations always being relative, in the sense that only the changes are noticed. She was puzzled, because if she looked around she could see all non-moving objects like the television, table, paintings, pots and vases, couches, chairs, appliances and hundreds of things in the room. She was not too sure why is seeing all of them not an observation.

I told Neera, "You look around and you see all objects. The process of seeing happens so fast that you need to slow down in order to comprehend it." When you are seeing in a direction, you notice something. This act of noticing happens in a small fraction of time when an image appears in the field of vision. The appearance of image is the change that you notice because something can only appear from its previous state of non-appearance. This change is being noticed by you. This quick appearance of an object in your observation is the movement we may call as attention. Let me explain in a few examples how the process of recognition of an object comes about in a slow-motion."

I gave Neera a few examples about observation of non-moving objects. In the first case, the eye movement caught the glimpse of flower port from top to bottom.

Attention begins on an object	
Attention starts capturing details	
Attention continues to capture details	
Attention catches the whole object(s)	
No more movement of attention	

Table: 2.1 Birth & End of Attention on stationary objects

In another example, I pointed out how something appears in awareness. It is similar to when you open your eyes and focus on something in front of you.

Attention begins on an object	
Attention starts capturing details	
Attention continues to capture details	
Attention catches the whole object(s)	
No more movement of attention	

Table: 2.2 Birth & End of Attention on stationary objects

In yet another example, I showed her how you capture some objects with a sweeping motion of your vision. A movement is always relative. A moving vision of a stationary object is same as a stationary vision of moving object.

Attention begins on an object	
Attention starts capturing details	
Attention continues to capture details	
Attention catches the whole object(s)	
No more movement of attention	

Table: 2.3 Birth & End of Attention on stationary objects

If I had to make note of something, I would have said that attention is a movement. Having an attention on an object is same as noticing the object. Losing attention on an object is also same as failing to notice the object, which happens when the object goes out of the field of observation.

Neera silently noted the finding in her notebook before continuing to ask for a clarification.

RULE 7: Attention is Movement.

She said. "I can understand now that appearing of an object in the field of observation or paying attention on an object can be seen as a movement. I can also figure out that a movement exists when the object goes out of the field of observation or when the attention is lost. But I am surprised why the observation happens only at the time of appearing or disappearing of non-moving objects, and should stop once an object is noticed completely?"

I said, "I didn't say that observation ceases after something is noticed. I said that the observation ceases after something is noticed and there is *no more movement*."

Neera still seemed confused.

I told Neera, "We already said that only changes are noticed. The observation is always on a movement. In absence of movement, there cannot be anything to observe.

Do you see the blank screen of a television? Can you continue to start on a blank wall? How long can you look at a perfectly clear sky with no trace of birds, clouds, planes or any other object? Can you hear a monotonous sound that doesn't change in pitch or frequency? How long do you continue to feel the touch of cold water when you jump in a swimming pool?"

Neera started to get a look of surprise on her face. "I never thought of that! Whenever there is something that doesn't change for some time, I start feeling that I am bored. I never thought it was because the movement is the basic need if the observation has to survive!"

I said, "You correctly said it."

Neera took out her notebook and wrote this.

RULE 8: There is no observation in absence of a movement.

I looked at my watch. It had been about an hour since we had started our discussion. The day had become warmer and it was not so pleasant to sit outside anymore. I wanted to wrap-up the discussion and wanted to check how much progress we made since we started. I asked Neera, "Can you please look at your notebook and tell me what we have figured out till now?" She said, "I don't need to look. I remember." Then she said that we had talked about all of the following by now.

Important things to know about Observation
- Point of observation, or an observer is always needed for a movement to exist
- Frame of reference is the point of observation
- To observe is to know
- Observer is the frame of reference
- Frame of reference, or the observer is non-moving
- In absence of observation, there is no observer; there is no movement

She said that we had discussed about all of the above points and really understood their validity, but was not sure about the last one. I told her that I remember her example of missing a day of school. Just because she didn't observe the activities going on at the school wouldn't mean that the teacher won't teach the class or if you sleep all day long the sun would continue to rise or set as it usually does.

I asked her, "Do you understand that the point of observation is always needed for a movement to exist?"

She said "Yes".

Then I asked, "Is the last point listed above not the same fact repeated in terms of negation?"

She said, "Yes, I do see that. But still I can't grasp it. This description is just as useless as the definition of a new word. Consider the fact that if I don't feel happy then you can't make me happy by telling all the reasons why I should be happy. I can understand that the movement is when observed. I can also see that the movement is a relative mechanism and a point of observation is essential. But to imagine that a thing or a movement does not exist if not observed is so lame!"

I said, "You are absolutely right. It is one of the most difficult things to understand. We will try to explore about this when we continue our discussion next time."

She looked tired. We had spent a whole hour discussing something that we always knew but never really explored. We never needed to. Nobody needs to. Just like every single piece of this universe is moving in the way that suits it best, we have also been moving, acting and living without ever realizing the immense beauty of the synchronicity. Every little particle moves; it moves in the way which suits it best; in the way that is the simplest way possible. A flowing river finds its way to the ocean. A bee finds its way to the flowers. Small ducklings don't have to be taught to follow their mother duck. A fish is never tired of swimming, or an ant of crawling, or a heart of beating endlessly. Everything in the universe has a peculiar nature, and there is no effort as long as the movement happens along with the nature. If we, as humans could figure out our real nature, we would be able to find the source of infinite energy, the energy that is so close to us, beating through heart or breathing through our lungs, and yet far and unknown.

Realm of Knowledge

*Neera wonders how her universe only
contains what she knows and nothing beyond*

"Papa, what is truth?" I heard Neera say.

It as a week since us two had talked. It was Friday evening, and I was relaxing on a couch, not doing anything in particular. For a few years, I was trying to reprogram myself, practicing the art of unlearning. We all have a few habits or urges that keep us busy. One such habit is to store every little thing in our memories that we observe. Continuing this way, we become a huge storehouse of countless memories and carry this burden of remembrances with us living endlessly. Having 'known' most of the things, our tendency to observe continues to diminish as perceiving can only happen on relative observation. Another such habit is to always find things to do that keep us busy or entertained. The urge to do something is the biggest source of our miseries. We cannot just do 'nothing'. If someone is asked to sit quietly and do nothing, that will the biggest punishment. The prisons are seen as the punishments because our normal tendency is to explore, find out, pursue and keep busy in doing something. A prison is an enforcement to ensure that you have no freedom to move or act for a prescribed period of time. In a pursuit to finding out our real nature, I sat my eyes towards trying to reverse this innate urge of doing something. A regular practice of meditation, studying various kinds of books on life, mind and philosophy, and spending most of time in investigating on the nature of life became my routine. So here I was, relaxing on the couch and really doing nothing when I heard Neera's voice.

> **Having 'known' most of the things, our tendency to observe continues to diminish as perceiving can only happen on relative observation.**

"Something that is not false". I replied when she asked me what the truth was.

"I am serious, Papa. I know what is not false is true. But for that we will have to know what false is."

"What do you think False is? You may have seen people lying many times. What is it that can be called a lie?"

"The only thing I can say about lie is that it is not true." She sounded confused.

"Would you want to explore on this yourself? I can suggest you something that you can do." I said.

"I would love to." She said expecting some excitement.

"Try to set up a survey with some of your friends or colleagues. Ask them to respond to a couple of your questions. When you have got the survey results, we can sit together and explore what is a truth or what is false."

"What kind of questions?" She asked.

"Let me think." I said. Then I spent a few minutes thinking about what simple question could be framed so that everyone finds it easy to answer without affecting the quality of results we wanted to achieve. I quickly drew a sketch and edited using a basic picture editor. I asked Neera to take her blue cap and the color pencil box with her when taking the survey. I wrote the following set of questions for her survey.

Neera's Truth / Falseness Survey:
1. Please give one true and one false answer to the question: What is the color of my cap?
2. In the following picture, color one section that is not an apple.

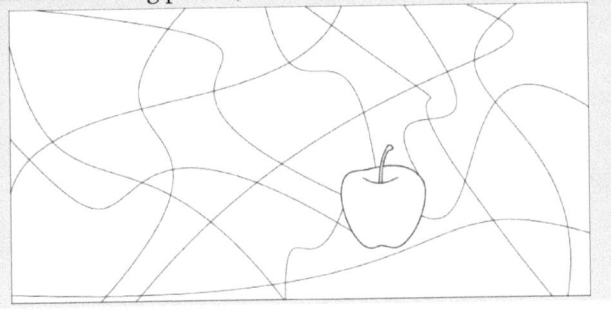

I waited for her to say anything but she didn't. She took the paper and kept it in her bag. She said, "I will try to get as many responses as possible over the next few days. My music class is on Tuesdays and Thursdays, and my PE (Physical Education) classes are on Fridays, so I should be able to get most of the responses by the end of the week." She looked happy. She always liked doing activities in groups and looked forward to be able to meet and talk to different students in her class. I saw that she was still sitting there as if she was waiting for something. After some time she spoke, "Papa, are you short?"

I said, "Yes, looking at the average height of people around us, I can be called short. Why do you ask?"

She said, "I never knew that. In fact, I never thought about you in terms of being short or tall. When I think of you or mom, this idea of height was never a reality. It was a strange experience today. A new student joined the class. In recess he was introduced to me. He is a good basketball player; a very tall person. When he met me he made a remark that I was quite short. He then said it might be because my dad might be short too. I said I didn't think so. I assumed that being short might not be a normal thing, and I never noticed anything unusual about you, so I didn't think you were short. At that time I saw my friends laughing. They told him that in fact my father was short too. I can still not believe that I never knew this before today, and everybody had known it all the time.

I told her, "I was always short. But you never knew it before today. The very fact about my height in comparison to other people was not a part of your knowledge. Something that you never knew or observed did not exist for you. Now that today you have been made to notice, you know that it is a fact. Is this not the last item from our list from previous discussion that you weren't sure about? You were not sure how a *movement did not exist if not observed*? Is it not what has happened with regards to my height? It was never known to you, so it never existed. It is only when you are made to notice that you have encountered a new fact. I have always been short, but for you it was not the part of reality, as it was never known. I hope you remember that *to observe is to know*."

She said, "I guess this is how it happened. But I am not sure if it applies everywhere and in all cases. If you remember, I told you that if I don't go to school tomorrow, the school will run, the teacher will teach the class even though I fail to observe anything. Things will exist even if I don't observe."

I said, "You know that the sun will rise tomorrow because it has been rising ever since you have known. You know that the teacher might come to class because you have known this happening since long. You know about these movements because they have already been observed by you. Is it possible for you to know what color clothes will she be wearing? If for some reason your teacher came in T-Shirt and Jeans for the first time ever, and you happened to have missed the class, would you ever know this? If someone tells you later that she saw the teacher wearing Jeans, you would never believe it. For you that is something impossible. You have not seen her in jeans all your life, and you cannot imagine her wearing jeans. This fact will be impossible for you. *Something that has not been observed by you has not happened* from your frame of reference."

She was listening carefully, trying to absorb.

I continued, "You would think that you would have heard of the richest person in the world. When I grew up, I heard of Bill Gates. I would find some news articles or television news talking about him. When I came to USA and in a small get-together, one of my friends started talking about a person called Warren Buffet. I did not find the discussion worth paying attention because I didn't have any clue about the person he was talking about. Then suddenly he mentioned that Mr. Buffet was the richest person in the world. It came to me as a total surprise. How someone could be the richest person in the world and I never knew? It looked as if he was making things up. I became interested in hearing more, so that I could find out if there was some amount of truth in his talks. He mentioned that a single stock of his company was about $100,000, and that those who owned even a few Stocks of his company were millionaires. Everything that I heard seemed more and more fake to me. How could there be a company with a

What I had never observed did not exist. What did not exist for me was not even the truth.

stock price of $100,000? What I had normally observed in the past was that companies had the habit of splitting their shares once they became expensive. When the discussion continued for more than an hour, I started thinking that there might be a little chance that all this might be true. When I returned home from the party, I went straight to my computer and searched for a few words such as 'hathaway' and 'buffet'. I could not believe that each and every word that was spoken that night was real. Before that day, there was no company called Berkshire Hathaway and no Billionaire called Warren Buffet in my observation or experience. What I had never observed did not exist. What did not exist for me was not even the truth."

Neera was silently listening.

I said, "Do you recall the example of two boats that I gave you last time? Each of the boats knows about the movement of other boat relative to themselves. They have no means of knowing their true course in the vast ocean in absence of any other fixed point of reference. The only way a boat can figure out where it is moving is by referring to something that is not moving. For this purpose, the navigators used the compass, which points to the directions according to the magnetic fields of the earth. The movement of the boat when observed from the frame of reference of the compass or the earth's magnetic field, is the movement of the boat with as observed by the non-moving observer, the earth itself.

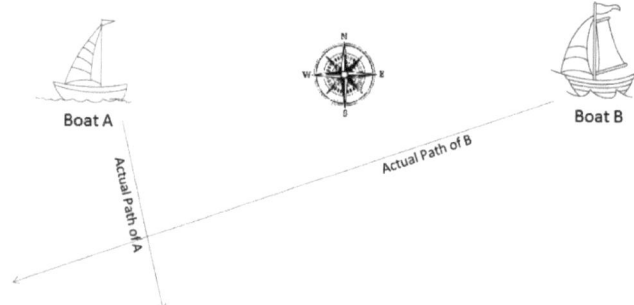

Picture: 3.1 A fixed reference establishes actual movement

Neera said, "I can see how logical this is. But I find it hard to believe it when you say that a movement does not exist if not observed."

I asked, "Do you know how much your mother hates the spiders".

She replied, "Oh, she totally hates the spiders. The first thing she will do is to throw it out of the house."

I asked her, "Last time when we saw the spider on the vase, why didn't your mother throw the spider away? You saw that we two were sitting here having our tea together."

She said, "Probably she didn't notice".

I asked her, "You said that she hates spiders so will always ensure that they are thrown out of the house."

She said, "That is true. She has to notice a spider before she throws it away".

> "You said that something that you don't know doesn't exist. But we know that the spider existed. Both of us saw it."

I said, "Is it not we are trying to say when we say that a movement has to be observed in order to know about it. And as long as we have not observed it, there is no way of knowing about it. Something that we don't know doesn't exist for us."

She said, "It is the last part that doesn't make sense. You said that something that you don't know doesn't exist. But we know that the spider existed. Both of us saw it."

I asked, "Have you ever seen a bench with a note saying that the paint is wet?"

She nodded.

I asked, "Can you know by looking at it if the paint is still wet?"

She said, "I don't think so. Paint normally takes a few hours to dry up completely. I can be sure if I can figure out that it has been long enough since it got painted."

Picture: 3.2 The sure way to know that a paint is wet is by touching it

I asked, "How would you know for sure if the paint is dry if you don't know how long ago was it painted?"

She said, "I will probably touch it to find out."

I asked, "How did we define observation at the very beginning?"

She said, "To observe is to know, which can be by means of seeing, hearing, smelling, tasting or touching."

I said, "So you are not sure about the movement of paint from being wet to being dry unless you have had an observation. This observation could be in terms of length of time since it was painted, or by the sense of touch. Once observed, you immediately 'know' about the paint being wet. Unless observed, the knowledge of movement is not available. If the knowledge of something is not available, that thing doesn't exist for us."

She said, "You made a different statement. It sounds like the key to understanding this difficult phenomenon."

I asked, "What? I am not sure what I just said".

She replied, "You said, that a thing exists if its knowledge exists. I am sure we could also say that a movement exists if its knowledge exists. If knowledge about something doesn't exist, the thing doesn't exist too. Yes, it seems to fit everywhere. You didn't have the knowledge about Mr. Buffet, so he didn't exist for you for most of your life. If I have no knowledge of my teacher wearing jeans on a particular day, it is as if it never happened for me. If I failed to observe or notice the sign on the freshly painted bench, the knowledge about the paint being wet will not exist for me. I might as well sit on the bench and spoil my clothes, something I would never do when aware of the fact."

Neera continued, "It is like someone trying to make fun of a blind person by making funny faces and strange gestures. The blind person will be totally unaware of this. With no knowledge of someone making faces, the possibility of any such movement does not exist for him. He will continue to be ignorant of this activity going on right in front of him. On the other hand, if he gets a chance to touch the other person's face and notices through touch that he is making funny faces, this behavior will become known for the blind."

I said, "You have said it right. Do you know how the big organizations work? They have a hierarchy where a number of employees report to a supervisor or a manager. Many such supervisors or managers report to another manager and so on building a pyramid with only a few people at the very top. Those top managers are responsible for taking actions on behalf of the whole organizations. Can you imagine how they observe changes or movements happening in and around the company? The only way a manager at the top can know about employees or their work at various levels is through the managers in the line of reporting. The supervisors or managers will know only as much as has been told or reported to them. If something has not been reported to them, they will never know. It is like something that doesn't exist. The knowledge available to the top management of a company depends on the efficiency of communication among its intermediate supervisors and managers."

I asked Neera, "So, can you say now what knowledge is?"

She said, "I remember. We already said, to observe is to notice, to know."

I was happy that she got this difficult idea cleared up. I said, "Observation is the key to all movements. To observe is to know. A movement doesn't exist before an observation; and once observed, a natural action is bound to happen based on the movement"

She waited to finish writing in her notebook before coming back with a reaction to my statement. She wrote her new discovery.

RULE 9: There is no movement in absence of an observer.

As soon as she finished writing, she asked me, "What did you mean when you said that once observed, a natural action is bound to happen?"

I said, "Remember this. I will explain when we talk next time."

4

Nature of Truth

The truth which has always been there and
yet far away from our observation; or is it so?

It was the election time and on different occasions, people were seen engaging in discussions passionately defending their choices of presidential candidates. Television channels were showing debates of both candidates on scheduled times. One evening Neera asked me if I was watching the debates. I replied that I had no particular interest in the elections. She was surprised by my indifference, and persuaded me to watch one that was due to happen in a couple of hours. I casually listened to her and chose not to think too hard about this. Soon she left to her room and I was left alone. In about an hour, I thought of doing something for the first time; that is to watch and hear the presidential debates. I switched on the television which had not been turned on for at least a few weeks. Not that I was completely cut off from the entertainment. I would occasionally watch a movie when it seems to be the one recommended by friends or critics.

After some initial formalities and introductions, the debate started and I forced myself to listen to the candidates alternately taking turns stating and defending their opinions, plans and strategies while contesting the opposite person. Within a matter of an hour, I started feeling tired of their speeches; they were either too mechanical or very unreliable. Here were two candidates, trying to become the leader of a strong country, and all I could hear in their communication was disagreement to what was being said by the other.

When one person commented something about the other, the other said, "No, it's a lie". Later when the other person reminded the former making some statement in past which happened to be proved wrong, the former denied, saying "That is not true. I never said that". I was wondering what exactly I was going to understand about these two candidates who are not even trustworthy! The whole debate did not seem to move beyond what was true or what was a lie. I switched the television off as it served absolutely no purpose trying to decipher anything useful out of the debates.

The same weekend, Nikka saw me and thought it was the right time to spend on continuing our discussion. The moment she came to me, she told me that her friend Nicole was very depressed. Nicole had a very good friendship with one of her classmates, Samantha. Not a day would go when they would not be seen together. Neera said that Nicole had recently found out that Samantha had been stealing things from Nicole for so many years. She had been missing some of her favorite belongings occasionally over the years, but attributed the losses to her carelessness. She has been heartbroken since the day she accidentally found the hidden side of Samantha. It came to her as a real shock as she could never imagine such a friendly and trustworthy person to have cheated her for so long.

"This is really sad." I said.

"Are you not surprised that someone could do something like this to their best friends?" She asked.

I said, "I am always surprised by such acts of people, but having seen so many instances like these, I have started learning about the ways things happen in this universe. Didn't I tell you last time that *there is no movement in absence of an observer?* Nobody saw Samantha steal things from Nicole, so the fact that Samantha could be a thief didn't exist. The only reality was that she was Nicole's good friend. It is only after something is observed that the new fact gets established. Had she never found this new information by chance, Nicole would always have known Samantha to be the best friend and a dependable person."

"I guess you are right. *If something is not observed, it does not exist.*" She said.

She suddenly changed topic and said, "You know what, I have some survey results on the two questions about truth and false. Do you have time to look at them?"

I was eagerly awaiting those anyway. I said, "Sure, we can see if they tell us something useful".

She brought a bundle of sheets and put them on table. Before I could say anything, she said, "These are all the responses that I got from my colleagues. I have noted the results in my notebook."

She showed her notebook with following result of her survey to the first question:

Question 1: What is the color of my cap? Give one true and one false response.

True	False								Total
Blue	Green	Yellow	Red	Pink	Black	Brown	Purple	Other	
49	12	8	11	3	4	6	2	3	49

I asked Neera, "Do you want to tell me what these answers tell you?"

Neera looked at her notebook and thought for some time. She said, "Well, everybody said my cap was blue when responding truly."

I nodded while waiting for her to say more.

She continued, "And there were all sorts of answers for the false response."

I asked, "What does it say about the nature of truth and falseness?"

She was confused. "I don't know what you are asking me." She said.

I said, "Let me tell you what I see in these responses. Then let me know if you too agree."

I continued, "You asked forty nine students to tell the truth about the color of your cap. All of them gave the true answer that the color of the cap was blue. What do you think the answers will be if you ask the same question to another hundred people?"

She said confidently, "They all will say the same thing, undeniably".

I further asked, "And what if you asked the question to a million people?"

She said, "Papa, it is obvious. As long as people are asked to give a truthful response, everyone will say that the color of the cap is blue, unless someone is color blind."

I said, "You saw that everyone says the same thing irrespective of how many people you ask for the truth. Can we say that truth is one and only one?"

She said, "I think we can".

I said, "You asked the question over a week and saw that the answers remained the same. If you ask another million people, I hope you would agree that the answer will still remain the same even if it takes you fifty years to do so. Can we not also say that the truth does not change over time?"

She said, "We can definitely say that too!"

I asked, "What do you say about something that does not change?"

She replied, "Constant, permanent, non-moving?"

I nodded in agreement.

I asked her. "Can you try to define what 'truth' is now?"

She said, "Truth is one. It is constant, permanent and does not change."

I asked her, "Let's explore about the false responses. What can we say about them?"

She said, "It seems that false replies were changing. They were many different kinds too."

I asked her, "Can you try to tell what it tells you about the nature of falseness, just the way we figured out about the truth?"

She was excited, "It is so straight-forward! Unlike the truth, the falseness is not one, but many. It is not fixed, but keeps on changing. Just as the truth is permanent, falseness seems temporary."

I was glad that she said it precisely. I asked her a final question, "Now that you have defined the truth, and the falseness, what do you think is the relation between the two?"

She seemed confused. "I am not sure what do you mean by the relation between the two." She said.

I said, "One is permanent and the other is temporary. One is singular while other is countless. One is permanent while the other is temporary. One does not change while the other is always changing form. What do you think is the relation between the two?"

She said, "Oh, I see! They are clearly the opposites."

I asked her, "Are they truly opposite; complementary? Is it ever possible to have an area of doubt where something could be between the two?"

She said, "There cannot be! They are totally separate. One is single while other is not. What could be between the two? Or what could be a doubtful state between temporary and permanent? Anything that ceases to be permanent will always be temporary. Anything that is not singular will always be non-singular. No, there is no doubt that they both seem to be totally opposites."

I asked her, "Could we then say, Truth is the opposite of False?"

She said, "Definitely."

I asked her, "Could we also say that truth is something not false. False is something not true?"

She nodded in agreement. She seemed pleased with the way we were able to come up to something so simple, yet so concrete. What seemed to be a complex question initially had finally been reduced to such a simple concept. A truth is simply 'one'. A truth is something permanent. A truth is something that never changes. If we look around, everything is moving, changing shape. There are some things which change thousands of times within a second, whereas there are other things which change a little in million years. Nevertheless, nothing ever remains same; so it seems! *Everything known must be false!*

She asked me, "Papa, this is absurd! If I start thinking, there is hardly anything that can be called true! Do you mean that everything that we see, hear or know is false?"

I said, "The answer to this question is not easy. We will have to explore some more before we can figure out more about what is truth and where is it found."

She seemed lost. A moment earlier she was excited that we had figured out a simple definition of truth and falseness.

A few minutes later, she was struggling to find out in reality what exactly would be seen as the truth.

She asked, "Papa, where can the truth be found? Everywhere I see, I see things that were not around at some point of time. When everything is temporary, what is that which can be called permanent?"

I told her, "You are confused because you are asking wrong question. Try asking something else."

She replied, "What else could I ask?"

I said, "You could ask, where the truth can be found?"

She said, "But I don't see how would this make it any simpler? I don't know where I can find it."

I said, "Try to remember what the truth is. Is it not something that is not changing, not temporary?"

She agreed.

I asked her, "If something is not changing and not temporary, is it possible for it to be present sometime and not some other time?"

She said, "If something is present at some time but not at other time, it has to be changing or temporary. Since the truth is not temporary, it has to be present all the time."

I asked her again, "If something is not changing and not temporary, is it possible for it to be present at some place and not at other place?"

She said, "If something is present at some place but not at other place, it cannot be called constant. Since the truth is constant and non-moving, it has to be present at all the places."

I repeated what she just said, "We agree that the truth is present at all the places all the times, constant and non-moving. Can this presence be known by any means such as seeing, hearing, touching, smelling, tasting, feeling or interpreting?"

She thought for a moment and then asked, "How can something be seen or heard if it has always been there at all the places not changing or moving? We had discussed that a movement is a relative phenomenon. We can only observe if something moves, something that changes, something that is differentiated from other, something that deviates from something else based on place and time. Something non-moving, non-discriminating can never be observed because *there cannot be an observation in absence of a movement* (Rule:8)."

I was excited, "You have become wiser." I said.

She was happy that she was able recall one of our previous learning. But she suddenly realized the trap. She said, "Truth is non-moving, permanent and constant. In absence of any movement there could never be an observation of truth. Don't you think we came to a dead end? A truth is something which can never be observed. Can it never be known? Is falseness and lies the only thing worth knowing?"

I said, "Don't be too hasty. Maybe this is not it means."

She asked, "What else does it mean? If truth cannot be observed, what use is there to explore about the nature of truth?"

I said, "You already said it in your question. We started to explore on the nature of the truth to become wiser. Have we not become wiser by knowing that the truth is not something that can be 'known'?"

She was not happy. She asked, "What good is the wisdom to know that there are things that can never be known?"

I asked, "Do you know that you can't fly?"

She said, "Yes, I know that humans cannot fly because their bodies are not made suitable for flying".

I asked her, "Does it help one to know that one cannot fly?"

She said, "Yes. If someone is stupid enough not to know that one cannot fly, one might attempt to jump off a high cliff trying to imitate the birds".

I asked her, "Do you know that you cannot eat peanuts?"

She said, "Yes, My body is allergic to nuts. Don't you remember I had to spend two days in hospital when I first ate peanuts from my friend's lunch box?"

I asked her, "You know that you cannot eat peanuts. Does it help to know this?"

She said, "Definitely, knowing that I am allergic to peanuts and I cannot eat them helps me remain safe."

I asked, "Is knowledge of the fact that you cannot fly, wisdom to you?"

She said, "Yes".

I asked, "Is knowledge of the fact that you cannot eat peanuts without getting sick, wisdom to you?"

She nodded again.

I asked, "Is knowledge of the fact that the truth can never be known, wisdom to you?"

She was quiet. She saw the logic. She knew that it was not useless to have known at least something about the nature of the truth. She was not yet sure, how this could be the wisdom, though.

I continued, "When you know you can't fly, you don't try to fly."

"..and in the same way you don't try to eat peanuts, when you know you cannot eat peanuts", I said.

I went on to finish it logically, "We have thought over, contemplated, and understood that the nature of truth is such that even though it is always present everywhere all the time around us, it cannot be known the way we know things around us. All the means of perception available to us cannot help in observing the truth, because *observation can only happen when movement happens* (Rule:8). Having known that the truth cannot be found, we stop. We stop looking at truth the way we look for things around us. We stop searching; seeking."

Neera asked, "I am not sure if this is true. We know that we cannot fly like birds. It is true that we became wiser and do not attempt to jump off the cliff. But that didn't mean we stopped trying to find other means of flying. We would never have invented airplanes if that was the case."

I was glad that she brought that up. I said, "Exactly!"

Neera was confused. She asked, "But isn't this just the opposite of what you just mentioned? You said we stop trying when we find something cannot be done."

I said, "I said we stop looking at the truth the way we look for things around us."

She continued to look at me. She knew that I must have something more to add to that.

I said, "Having known that humans cannot fly like birds, humans didn't try to continue jumping off the cliffs flapping their arms like birds. They invented planes or gliders that could fly like birds and carry their bodies with them. In the same way, once we know it completely that truth is not something that can be known, we stop interpreting the nature of truth just the way we try to interpret and understand all other things in the world. We do something else!"

She was quietly listening.

I said, "There is a truth, and then there is everything false. You know that the truth is constant, ever present, non-moving entity that cannot be perceived through the means commonly used by humans. Everything that is perceived is a relative movement sensed by one or more of the sense organs available to human beings as well as every other living organism in this universe."

I then asked Neera, "Did we not already figure out from our survey about the nature of truth being exactly complementary to everything false?"

She said, "Yes. We did".

I asked Neera. "Did we not have two different set of problems on our survey. Can you show me how did the coloring page come about?"

Neera grabbed the sheet from her bundle of papers and showed me the picture which was colored by different participants. They were asked to color a section in the picture that was 'not an apple'. The picture looked like this.

Picture:4.1 The composite colored 'not apple' section contains all the information available in the 'apple'

I told Neera, "Did we not ask everyone to color something *not an apple*?"

Neera said, "Yes, this is what we asked and this is exactly what they all did".

I asked her, "If apple is the truth, what does *not an apple* mean?

Neera said, "If apple is the truth, then not an apple is false".

I asked, "Can you say that this picture been colored at every single area known to be false?"

She said, "Yes. We have covered everything that is false".

I asked her again, "If you ignore everything false on this picture, what are you left with?"

She said, "The only area left uncolored is the apple, the truth."

I said, "We cannot perceive the truth. But we can perceive everything false. In other words, everything we ever perceive is always going to be the false according to the very nature of movement being a *change in place and time*".

She nodded in agreement.

I asked her, "What did we figure out when we get rid of everything that we know to be false?"

Neera said, "If everything false is gone, we are left with the truth."

I summarized, "Is it not then, the way to go about finding the nature of the truth? Since we cannot perceive the truth directly, we must go on rejecting everything that is false. We don't care what the truth looks like, smells or tastes like. All we know that whatever we see, hear or do is not the real truth. We continue to ignore everything that is temporary, whether pleasures, pains, sorrows or our achievements as they are nothing but movements on the screen of life. We continue living our lives constantly aware of our being on the side of the truth always, because when everything that is false is ignored, nothing but the truth remains."

5

Observation and Action are One

The source of infinite energy, the right kind of action depends on the right observation.

The summer had officially started and the afternoons were unbearably hot. The evenings were still pleasant and I used to enjoy a lazy walk by the lake in the neighborhood park every day. One day when I came home after my walk, I found Neera in the family room. She was casually flipping through a science magazine. I asked her, "How come you are not in your room today?" She said, "I just got my finals finished today." I understood. Every time her exams finished, she would get a break from her busy life and breathe some air of relief at least for a few days. I went to the kitchen and started making my tea. After putting the mixture of water and milk to boil, I went on to add sugar and tea. As I was about to get a spoon from the kitchen drawer, my eyes got a glimpse of some movement in the corner of the drawer. I noticed that it was a scorpion. I stopped what I was doing and pulled the drawer carefully out of the cabinet. The drawer was heavy due to lot of steel cutlery and needed to be lifted with both hands. As I approached the family room, I asked Neera to open the main door. She looked and immediately asked, "Scorpion?"

In Arizona, it is quite common to find scorpions in and around the houses. The common variety is a bark scorpion whose sting is not lethal but still quite painful. It had become a routine for us to occasionally spot a scorpion in the house and then carry them outside our house and leave them out in the open at some safe distance from our house. I carried the whole drawer out of the house and carefully emptied its contents till there was only the scorpion left. I flipped the drawer on the ground and let the scorpion leave by itself. I put back the entire cutlery in the drawer and returned. When I came to the kitchen I saw that the milky water in the pot had been boiling for a long time without any sugar or tea. In the whole drama escorting the scorpion outside, I had totally forgotten that I was preparing my tea. I added some more water and milk with the sugar and tea because most of liquid was lost boiling. In a few minutes, I got my tea into a cup and came back to the family room where Neera was still lazily sitting doing nothing.

There are many ways people react when sighting a scorpion. Giving out a loud shriek is one of the most common one. Some squash them right away under their foot while some other may try to grab something to hit them. It is quite customary for some people to go out in the backyard at night with ultra-violet black light torch to hunt for scorpions. The bodies of scorpions are such that when the black light from UV torch falls on them, they give out a neon blue illumination. People with small kids in the house do not want to take any chances as a scorpion bite to a child could be dangerous. Many people put a sticky tape at the bottom of the main entry doors of the houses. Scorpions get stuck to those tapes and can't get away. It is quite common for people to use diatomaceous earth powder. They sprinkle the power where it's probable for the scorpions to crawl. The powder gets coated on their bottom of the bodies and kills them by dehydrating them slowly. Whatever means people may employ when it comes to responding to scorpions, but in no case will someone ever ignore one if it is observed. You may chose to ignore a common house lizard or a spider, but not a scorpion.

While I spent a few minutes relishing the hot tea, Neera was busy going over the few magazines that were lying on the center table. When she saw that my tea had finished, she looked at me and said, "Papa, we had started our discussion about movements and observation. Later we had gone over understanding the nature of truth. I am not sure if I can see if any of the things that I have come to know about observation and movement helps me understand the world any better. Am I too dumb to apply what I already understood intellectually?"

I said, "No. You are not dumb. Actually we have hardly covered the basic principles of movement. It is when you understand the whole sequence of observation, movement and action; you will begin to appreciate how things move around."

She asked, "A sequence of observation, movement and action? I am not sure what that is."

I replied, "Observation of the movement is only half of the story; an incomplete story. In nature, nothing is incomplete. Every observation has to be followed by an appropriate action."

Neera said, "Let's slow down. I am not sure I understand exactly what you mean. I don't want to miss something useful that you might have said."

She started asking me one question at a time, "What happens when a movement is observed?"

"Action" I said.

"What kind of action?" She asked.

"An action that is appropriate to the observation." I replied.

Neera said, "Let's see. At first we said that there is no movement if there is no observation. Then later we also said that there is no observation in absence of a movement. Now we are saying that there is an action appropriate to the observation."

I said, "Precisely. An appropriate action pairs up with the observation. The observation-action pair acts like a unified force, an unlimited energy."

Neera tried to understand what I was saying. She tried to rephrase, "You mean to say that not only is the observation-movement an incomplete event, but its pairing up to an appropriate action is a must, and is possibly an event involving unlimited energy!"

I asked, "You said it right, but do you understand it?"

Neera replied, "Obviously not. What do you mean by unlimited energy? We has never studied in schools anything about energy being unlimited."

I asked, "Are you breathing right now?"

She said, "Of course, I am breathing right now. Every living being breathes oxygen lest it dies."

I asked, "How long have you been breathing?"

She said, "Forever; since I was born."

I asked, "You have been breathing forever days and nights; don't you get tired of breathing?"

She said, "No. It comes naturally. I don't think anybody ever gets tired of breathing."

I asked, "What can you say about the energy that drives the breathing in our bodies. Isn't this an unlimited source of energy that doesn't ever let you feel tired?"

She said, "Since I have always been breathing effortlessly, I never thought that there must have been some source supplying me this abundant energy. Now that you mentioned, I remember I easily get tired trying to inflate a few balloons by blowing air. Whereas when it comes to inflating my own lungs, I never get tired. This is absolutely amazing!"

I said, "So you do agree now that there is a possibility of a source of unlimited energy available to every living creature in this universe".

She said, "Yes, I can see. Every creature has been breathing air throughout its life effortlessly."

I said, "And you must also know that our hearts have been continuously pumping blood, pushing it through millions of tiniest arteries and veins forever.

She said, "Yes. We have studied it in our biology class."

I asked, "Do you know we have two pumps in our swimming pool. They run about six hours every day pumping water through the pipes and filter assembly. They get hot, break down many times and need a lot of energy in terms of electricity bills?"

She said, "I didn't know that. I only enjoy the clean pool. I don't know what goes on in making it sparkling clean".

I said, "I am trying to say that every little process needs some form of energy to drive it. When things continue to move, they get tired. We too get tired after continuously moving and acting all day. But nobody ever gets tired of breathing or beating of one's own heart. It may happen in some cases when bodies develop some ailment in form of asthma or heart issues, but not in otherwise heathier bodies."

Neera questioned, "I can see what you mean by unlimited energy. Are you implying that the same unlimited energy that seems to operate our bodies through breathing or beating our hearts is also driving our movements?"

I said, "Yes, this is what it looks like."

Neera said, "Let's go back to what you were saying when I interrupted you about the unlimited energy. You were saying that observing a movement is a partial, incomplete thing, and there must be an appropriate action based on the observation. I don't understand why there must always be an action."

I asked her, "Do you remember our first discussion about the nature of movement when we had spotted a spider on the vase?"

She said, "Yes, I remember."

I asked her again, "and what did you say your mom would do when she comes to *know* of a spider in the house?"

She said, "I said mom cannot tolerate spiders. The moment she spots one, she will stop everything she is doing and ensure first that the spider is out of the house."

I said, "You mean that once your mom spots a spider, an appropriate action is a must!"

I saw a sparkle in her eyes, "Oh! I know what you mean when you say that an appropriate action must follow. Just like the spider MUST be out once noticed."

Then she asked, "But we both also observed the spider. Why is there no action with our observation?"

I said, "This is why we talked about appropriate action. What is appropriate action for your mom spotting a spider is not what an appropriate action is for us. Ignoring something is an action too, which we did in this case."

Neera seemed confused. "How is it useful to know about this the whole observation-action sequence, when anybody could take any action on an observation?"

I said, "The first thing to know is that the observation always pairs up with an appropriate action. Then we should know that the action which gets generated out of a response to an observation has a potential to possess an unlimited energy. It depends on the observer and the quality of observation that decides what kind of action happens.

Then I asked, "If there are ten boxes, and only one of them contains some money, which one will you be interested in?"

She responded, "The one with the money. Why would I care about all those boxes which don't have anything useful?"

I said, "The same way, out of several occasions of not so appropriate action following an observation, we are interested in the one with infinite energy. Remember, we are interested in finding out the mysteries of the universe, about the movement that goes on every moment in every single place! In the process of our exploration, we will continue to focus on things that interest us the most, while ignoring anything less promising."

Neera was listening. I continued, "When there is a cow with its belly full, it will ignore another bundle of straw being put in front of it. It will sit lazily without reacting to the food being placed in front of her. The action that is happening at this time from the perspective of the cow is of ignoring the food. We don't want to waste our time on thinking about the uselessness of observation-action sequence where ignoring is the most appropriate action to the act of noticing. What we want to focus is on the immediate surge of energy that the cow gets when it notices an approaching wild animal, such as a tiger."

Neera said, "I understand now. I think I was confused because in the beginning we said that an appropriate action is a MUST. I thought, every action following an observation-movement sequence must be full of energy. It seems there are only a certain cases when the observation-action pair would involve unlimited energy. What could probably be the criteria of such actions?"

I said, "The cow which could probably have responded to the straw being offered as food, did not move because its belly was full. Maybe it doesn't find the idea of food rewarding enough at that moment. The same cow might immediately get up and run for its life when faced life threatening situation. Do you see the two kinds of forces that contribute to the movement, the action?"

Neera asked, "Is it reward and punishment?"

I said, "Correct; the reward is a force of attraction, whereas the punishment is the force of repulsion. Every creature avoids the pain of punishment and moves away from it. Every creature gets attracted to the joy of rewards, and moves towards it. These are the two basic forces which seem to move this universe. In their extreme sense, you could also call them as life and death."

Neera was quietly listening. She was curious to know what more was there for me to say.

I told her, "We know that the action that follows for your mother on seeing a spider is the one that completes the sequence of observation-action. What all can we say about such actions?"

Neera knew that I was asking her these questions to build on a general principle for such actions. It was not simply an ordinary discussion trying to kill some time discussing on random topics to satisfy our boredom. It was intended to go deep into the process to understand what could possibly be the way to understand and capture the source of unlimited energy that is so easily accessible to our bodies, and so mysteriously hidden from our minds.

Neera spoke after thinking for some time. She asked, "Isn't it immediate?"

I said, "Good. You are correct. We know that the observation (of a movement) is an incomplete piece; it gets completed only when an appropriate action follows. This action has to be immediate. There can be no time gap between observation and action."

Neera said, "This is really the case. When mom spots a spider, she drops everything she is doing immediately to take on the spider."

I said, "Do you know what happened this morning? When I was half way through making my tea, I spotted a scorpion in the kitchen. What followed next was nothing that

I did purposefully. I had completely forgotten about the tea and didn't care to check what clothes I was wearing. I did not lose time in thinking, but simply acted. This action was whatever was appropriate for me to get away from the current situation. There was never a time gap between noticing the scorpion and acting on it".

I then continued, "So, what else can we say besides the fact that the action is immediate?"

She said, "When you were talking about the spider, you mentioned that you forgot about the tea you were making or the clothes you were wearing. This shows that such action has a high degree of attention. The total focus is on the action."

I was glad that she had noticed the fine details. I asked her, "Yes. An unwavering determination or focus is another aspect of such actions. Can you say that this act was done with unlimited energy?"

She said, "Yes; an unlimited energy. Just like we go on breathing every moment without complaining of tiredness, you were completely attentive to the task of dropping Mr Scorpion out of the house. You didn't get tired, annoyed or waited for the event to end. In fact, there was no possibility of any such thoughts even entering your mind while you were busy undergoing the act. From the moment you noticed the scorpion till the moment you got hold of the situation, you were simply acting. You were acting as if something else was driving the whole action."

I said, "You worded it rightly. Such actions are driven by something else, something that could be the source of unlimited energy. This can mean that as long as we are trying to act on something based on our will, desire or a plan, we will continue to exhaust a lot of energy, getting tired in the process. Just like you trying to blow air in balloons."

I continued, "You know when your room is not tidy and your mom tells you to clean it up, do you do it immediately?"

Neera said, "No. I know I am messy; and lazy too. Mom has to repeatedly tell me many times to clean up my room. In the end she has to threaten me strongly to make me move. I am sorry; I will try to manage my area better."

I asked her, "You don't feel like cleaning up your room even when you are made to notice many times. But what happens when one of your friends calls you that they are coming to your house for some help with homework?"

Neera said, "Then my whole room and bathroom gets in perfect shape with the lightning speed."

I asked, "Where does your lazy body suddenly get energy from?"

Neera replied, "I don't know. But I can't stand the idea that I might be seen as a messy person by my friends."

I said, "So, the repeated warnings from your mother cannot make you do something, whereas just a simple call from your friend suddenly fills you with infinite energy."

Neera was quiet. She seemed to be getting the point I was trying to make. Each living entity in this universe has some sort of connection to the unlimited source of energy. That unbound energy continues to drive every movement from tiniest atoms to the biggest galaxies. Human minds may have grown a lot in terms of evolution, yet they are far from tapping the source of such energy. It is paradoxical that an effort to act intentionally will never achieve the kind of focus, immediacy, urgency or the unbounded energy that the right kind of observation or noticing can bring about. Neera was slowly getting acquainted to one of those little secrets of this wonderful universe.

I asked Neera, "Have you ever had a tooth pain?"

Neera said, "Yes. It was a horrible experience. I had to go to the dentist and get two of my wisdom teeth out."

I asked "When you had the tooth pain, did you do anything else such as watching movie, going out to your friends, or spending time on social media?"

Neera said, "From the moment I had the tooth pain, till I happened to meet the dentist, I had nothing else on my mind. The most important thing for me was that the pain should go. How could I think of watching television, movie or going out with my friends?"

I asked, "Can we say that noticing or observing a movement as severe as a tooth ache can force an action that is focused, immediate and total?"

Neera said, "I like the way you named such action. I might better call it a FIT action, for being Focused, Immediate, and Total which means having unbound energy."

I asked Neera, "I like it; FIT action! Can we both talk about a few more observation-movement sequences that result in a FIT action?"

Neera said, "Let me try to quote some. I normally go to sleep at night before 10:00PM. However, before every exam day, I pull out an all-nighter, which means that I don't go to sleep. I spend all my night studying. I don't know where I get all the energy and drive. Once the exam is over, I spend the whole next day sleeping."

I said, "That is quite an example of a FIT action. The happening of the exam is real, just like the tooth ache is real. The action that follows is immediate, focused and total."

Neera asked, "Do you think we could use this knowledge to be able to tap the unlimited energy available to us freely?"

I said, "Why not. Just put yourself into a tooth-ache like situation, and every time you will experience the timeless action. On the other hand, if anytime you try yourself doing any action, you will see its limitation in terms of lack of focus, immediacy and completeness."

I continued, "I remember a wise person used to tell about such actions. His name was Jiddu Krishnamurty, and he used to simply say, *"Observation is Action."* For a long time, I never understood how observation could be an action. I was trying to understand this message in literal sense, whereas he was trying to imply the power that lied in the observation, which had an infinite drive to feed the timeless action that followed."

Neera asked me, "Can I note this message down in my notebook even if it seems to have been suggested by someone else?

I said, "Why not! I am sure he wouldn't have minded as long as you were able to understand the message in its real sense, and not used it as a fun quote on some social media. But, before you do that, let's quickly do something else."

I thought this was the time to introduce Neera to the art of building upon the ideas using pictures. I asked her to use the previous model of observation using a comparator and add the idea of action following a comparison. She was intelligent and figured out what was being told to her. She added to the previous picture.

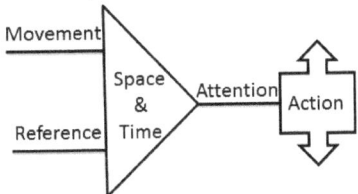

Picture: 5.1 Observation-Action Pair

I was satisfied with the model she drew. Seeing that I was satisfied with her noting, she continued updating her notebook with the quote that seemed too powerful to be ignored.

RULE 10: Observation is Action.

6

What movements are observed?

Neera gets to know the fundamental rules of observation of movements in this universe

It had been a few weeks since I and Neera had talked at length. She had been becoming increasingly busy with her schedules. She had signed up for Marching Band in her school which required her to wake up early at 5:00AM to reach for the morning sessions on time. She also had to attend evening practices every Wednesday and Friday from 7:00PM till 10:00PM. Every few months, they used to perform at a central location with all other school teams. There were about seventy different school teams and the program typically lasted all day till late night. The whole school campus used to be filled with hundreds of buses carrying the children and band equipment. It was not easy to easily find out where your child was practicing. Last week I had dropped her at one such event in the evening. She told me that I could come pick her up at around 11:00PM. It was a large gathering of students and I didn't want to get lost trying to find her in the middle of the night. I asked her to wait for me at the front gate, at such a place that I could easily spot her from the car when I come to pick her up. She agreed.

That night, at around 11:00PM she called me and said that she would be finished in about fifteen minutes. The place was about twenty minutes' drive from my place, so I started getting ready. When I reached the main entrance of the school, I tried to look through my car but could not spot her anywhere. After waiting for her for five minutes, I decided to park the car and walk inside the building. When I was about to enter the building, I got a call from her. She said, she was standing right at the corner of the front entrance as I had asked her to. I looked back and saw that she was standing under a tree in absolute darkness. I asked her how the program was and she said it was quite good. She was happy that her team had got sixth rank among all the teams.

While driving home, I told Neera that even though she stood outside the main entrance as I asked her to, she was barely visible to me. I said that she might have been able to see everything clearly standing in the dark place, but that didn't mean that others could also see her easily. Then I said to her, "It seems we need to talk more about how observation gets influenced in different situations. I hope you remember our discussion in the past about the movements and observation."

It seems she was waiting for me to bring this up. She said, "Papa, you told me that observation happens when movement happens. When I look around, everything is moving. When there is only one movement, I can understand that it might be possible to notice through senses such as seeing or hearing. But if there are two or more movements happening, which ones will be observed? Moreover, when we go outside on road, there are hundreds of things moving. In nature too, there are so many objects, sounds and smells. How does any living entity notice movements? Is there some ground rule for the observation to happen?

I said, "There has to be one. In fact, there is such a ground rule for observation. This rule is the basic rule that is working everywhere, all the time. The cosmos is in perfect synchronism due to the same reason."

Neera asked, "Why would the cosmos achieve perfect synchronism because of the ground rule for observation?"

I said, "If you remember we found out that observation and (further) action are not two independent acts but one complete process."

Neera nodded.

"If every piece of the cosmos follows a common ground rule of observation, then that observation is bound to initiate the appropriate movement. The movement so achieved will again be observed with the same ground rule. This is the never ending game that continues to be played on the backdrop of cosmos."

Neera asked, "Why should there be one common ground rule for all observation? Can different pieces not have different rules of observation?"

I said, "Everything in the nature is always changing. I am sure you must have read in your science class about evolution. What are land animals today might have evolved from fishes or aquatic animals millions of years ago. What is a leaf today will be decomposed and become part of dust. What is part of earth today will become part of some living being's organ. In other words, what is a leaf, is also the dust, is also the part of living beings. There is no actual division in nature. There cannot exist a way to have different rules when there is no firm demarcation between two things in the nature."

Neera was quiet. She had never thought so deep into anything. She said, "Everything does change and merges into another! I have always had this confusion in my mind. The tree in our backyard has shed all its leaves during this winter. Now it seems to have grown new leaves all over. If none of its original leaf are left, is it still the same old tree or is it a different tree?"

I said, "There cannot be an answer to this question that will satisfy you. The tree is not an object but a response of some process. You could call that process as treeing. The tree is the name we give to the response which appears in some unique pattern seen as a trunk, branches, leaves, flowers and fruits. If you look at every tree as the process of treeing, you would never ask this question. The process is same as the process of raining or rivering."

Neera said, "What is rivering?"

I said, "What you call a river is actually the continuous flow of water. Every moment the section of river you look at completely refreshes itself with new water. Yet we continue to identify a (flowing) river as a permanent object. Just like we see rain as raining, we might as well see a river as rivering, a process of continuous flow of water." There was actually no such word as rivering in the dictionary, but I thought it might make the comparison to be easily understood.

Neera said, "I would like you to talk about this more, but I know we were discussing about the ground rule of observation. I will remember to bring back this topic later."

"I can understand there are no two things in nature that have been, are and will continue to be totally independent of each other. This means that there cannot ever be a different rule for different things, because there are no exclusive different things in the universe." She added.

I asked Neera, "Do you remember what we said about the nature of the field of observation in the very beginning?"

Neera thought for some time, and then said, "We said that the frame of reference is the point of observation, a non-moving observer."

I said, "Right! The observer is non-moving, constant point of reference. There is no separation in various elements as the universe is always in a flux. Since there cannot exist different rules of observation from different perspectives, there has to be one universal principle of observation of movements. We need to explore what that ground rule is."

Neera asked, "If there was one, why hasn't anyone tried to figure this out? Why is this burden of figuring out the universal principle of observation on both of us suddenly?"

I said, "This rule comes so naturally that people don't even think they are following some rule. For example, if I tell you to close your eyes and try to point towards your toe, will it be difficult for you?"

Neera closed her eyes, pointed towards here toes and said, "There; It's right there".

I asked, "Can you try to figure out the ground rule about how you did it?"

Neera said, "Why should I? I can always point to any part of my body even without looking. I have always known it. I don't need to learn something when I already know it."

I said, "Maybe this is the reason nobody ever tried to figure out about the ground rules of observation. Observing came so naturally to everyone that they never thought they needed to know the details, just like you never need to know what goes on when you try to locate your body parts"

Neera said, "Fair enough. So here we are, trying to figure out something that nobody bothered to ponder over. But why should we? What do we gain by figuring out how things move around in the universe?

I replied, "We are part of this universe. We follow the same ground rules of observation (followed by an appropriate action) as anything and everything in the universe. If we can figure out the rules of observation, we can understand how we move and act. If we know about ourselves completely, we also know about everything else because the rules are same. By knowing this one thing, we know about the whole universe."

Neera was listening. She asked, "So what's the rule? Do we know this?"

I said, "Yes. We know the rule by heart. Everyone knows it. These rules are in fact, being used to control, regulate, influence and over-power everything and everybody in the universe by the humans.

Neera said, "Tell me about these rules. I want to know myself better. So I will eventually know everything else better."

By this time, we had reached our house. As we came in, I told her that it was already midnight and we could continue our discussion in the morning. She was tired after long hours of practice and went to sleep.

Next morning when I was having my tea, Neera came and asked if we could continue our discussion. I was waiting for her and had already thought out how I wanted to share this part of information with her. I opened the lid of my laptop computer and loaded one of the files I had been updating for quite some time. I said, "I will show you a couple of pictures. You have a look and tell me what the first thing you saw was."

I then showed her these two pictures.

Picture: 6.1 Different size of a word decides the priority of noticing it

She looked at the pictures and told me that the first thing she saw in the first picture was "Death". In the second picture, her attention fell on the word "Birthday". I asked her, "Why did you see these words first?"

"These words stand out. They are big." She said.

I asked her, "Is it a rule? Do big things always stand out in presence of all other things not as big?"

Neera said, "Sure, it seems like a rule. A bigger object gets attention in presence of other smaller object."

I asked, "We already said that attention is movement. Can we say that what applies to attention also applies to the movements universally as a ground rule?

Neera said, "Sure we can. It is so obvious. This is how it happens with everybody. Bigger things get noticed easily. On our birthday parties, I always see bigger pieces of cake get finished earlier as everyone grabs those first. In my fried rice plate, I can easily take out the pieces of peanuts because they are big and easily seen among hundreds of smaller pieces of rice."

I asked Neera, "When you have to sell your used books in your school and you are allowed to put an advertisement on the notice board, what would you do to make it easily seen among hundreds of other notices?"

She said, "I will use BIG words. They will be seen first among every other kind of message."

I asked Neera, "Does the rule apply only to vision or does it also apply to hearing?"

Neera asked, "What do you mean?"

I asked, "When you hear many voices together, which voice does your attention easily go to?"

Neera said, "The loudest one, obviously."

I said, "So the ground rule of observation is that a bigger movement gets *noticed* first, in presence of everything else not so big." I hoped that Neera paid attention to my stress on the word 'noticed'.

I asked Neera to bring some index cards and start writing the rules that seemed to evolve out of our investigation. She found the idea interesting. She went to her room and came with a stack of index cards. On the first one, she wrote this rule.

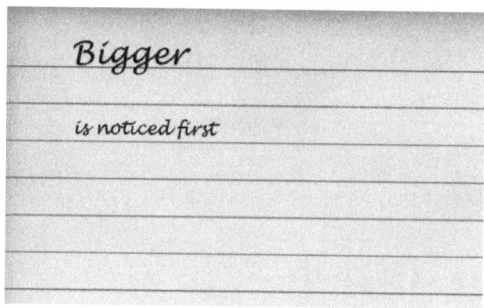

I saw that Neera was perplexed about being asked to bring index cards and note the findings on them rather than in her notebook. Nevertheless, she kept quiet.

I asked Neera, "Now that you have noted this down on the index card, let us look at some more cases. What do you see in this picture immediately? I showed her this picture from my laptop.

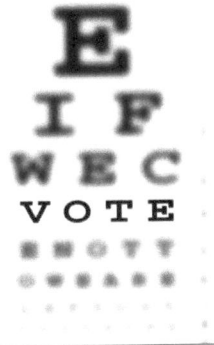

Neera said, "My attention is on VOTE."

I asked her, "But those four letters are not the biggest ones. The bigger ones are E, I, F, W, E and C. What do you think made you ignore all those bigger letters and bring your attention to the much smaller letters V, O, T and E?"

Neera said, "Those big letters are not sharp or as clearer as the smaller letters. The eyes seem to catch sharper image before any blurrier image even if the latter is bigger."

I was glad that Neera had picked up the right information out of the example. I wanted to see if she was able to apply this example elsewhere. I asked her, "It seems logical in this case. But do you see if this is really a rule that can be applied to different situations?"

Neera thought for a moment. She started thinking out loudly, "If eyes catch sharper images than the blurrier ones, then it should be easy to influence others to see things in a particular way. Who would want to influence people to view a picture in a certain way; a painter, artist, photographer?" There was a sparkle in her eyes. She had taken photography classes as one of the electives. She was taught on how to use focus on the intended object in a picture while leaving the background blurry. She tapped a few times on her phone and showed me this picture.

Picture: 6.2 The element in focus grabs the attention and stands out

I was impressed. She had brought out a very appropriate example. The picture had many things to look at, yet only one of the flowers was sharp and clear. When seen at first, the sharp image of the single flower becomes the center of attention leaving everything blurry to be ignored. I asked Neera, "Do you want to rewrite this finding on your index card?

Neera wrote a new message on the index card.

Neera told me, "I can see that there are going to be more example where something else is more important to clarity and bigger size. I am sure you are going to make me many more index cards."

I asked her, "As you have already guessed, can you think of any more attributes that help making something stand-out against all other things; something that makes an object prominent?"

Neera said, "We use all sorts of techniques that can make words, sentences, pictures or things to show up prominently. In a word editor, we can modify a few words or sentences to become bold, italic or underlined. In picture, we can highlight a part by making it brighter."

I showed her the same picture where the biggest word 'Birthday' was prominently catching the attention. When the words 'Memory' and 'Birth' were highlighted by making them bolder, they caught the initial attention even though they were smaller in comparison to many other words.

Picture: 6.3 Highlighted words are noticed before many bigger words

I asked, "Let us call all sort of accent as boldness. Where do you think the attention quickly falls on a picture containing various objects, some of them blurry, some focused, some big, some bold?"

Neera said, "I am not sure if sharpness takes a priority to boldness or the boldness takes a priority to sharpness."

I said, "I am not sure too. It depends. On objects that need clarity such as written words, the clarity takes precedence. On other things that do not need clarity, the boldness takes precedence. In a picture of a burning candle, the blurry but brighter lamp gets an attention to everything else sharper or not. In the interest of generic nature of rules for movement, we will ignore the use of language and need for things to be extra sharp. We will keep the boldness at higher priority to the sharpness of objects in the field of observation.

Neera tacitly agreed. She wrote on her third piece of index card.

Neera asked me, "Do you think what we are noticing about the nature of observation of movements is universally true? Does everything experience attention to movements in this particular manner? If it does, why should it be in this particular way and no other?

I asked Neera "What do you mean by the observation being in a particular way and not any other way?"

Neera asked, "For example, would a mouse not see a cheese even if it is *blurry*? Would an ant miss a particle of sugar if it was not *bigger*?"

I replied, "Are you sure the only aspect about *noticing* is through eyes? Did we not discuss that observation exists when *noticing* happens through any of the senses such as sight, hearing, smelling, touching and tasting? It may be true that the *sight* of a piece of cheese may be *blurry* for the mouse. It may also be true that the size of sugar particle may not be *big* enough to be *noticed* by an ant. But the sense of *smell* might be the *bold* enough to drive their attention towards their food. In the same sense, the strong sense of *touch* for a creeping plant might be the guiding force of movement allowing it to climb on the nearby solid structures such as poles, walls or trees."

I continued, "Though we are using examples mostly understood in human sense, we are trying to figure out if there exists a universal rule of observation. I am sure that if we are born with some basic knowledge then everything else is too. We humans cannot be naïve enough to believe that it is only our privilege to be able to see, hear or figure out various things while all other living beings are just too dumb to know or sense anything. What we understand to be true is not out of our (human) intelligence, but out of the same underlying intelligent rule that is guiding everything else in the universe."

I continued on to building a base for further ground rules, and said "If we fear death, so does any other living creature in this universe. If we desire food, shelter and safety, so does every other living creature. We try to avert pain and seek happiness, so does every other thing. How exactly are we separate from or different than the whole world out there? *We are what everything else is. Everything else is what we are.*"

Neera said, "I think this is how everyone behaves. No one likes pain. Everyone fears death. Given a choice, everyone chooses lesser pain."

I said, "There is no denying that all living entities avoid pain. It is also true that every living being avoids death. It seems logical that the pain and the death are seen similar in the sense of taking an action.

Neera asked, "Does it not mean that it becomes a rule for the *appropriateness* of an *action* following an observation?"

I was glad that she caught that right away. "Yes, an *appropriate action is the one that allows an entity to move away from pain, or death.* A movement towards lesser pain is the obvious choice when someone is in a situation of bigger pain."

Neera recognized the underlying force that seemed to guide an appropriate action when a movement was observed. She recorded this most important and basic rule in her notebook.

RULE 11: All movement is away from death.

As long as an entity is living, everyday decisions are derived from the same underlying force which makes every living creature strive for a life away from its destruction. The pain is an indication of something destructive and every living being is 'programmed' to avoid pain which ultimately seems to take it away from a possible death like situation. It was like a rule.

RULE 12: Pain is like Death.

Once a feeling of pain is associated as a destructive force, the inherent programming makes it behave as if facing a death like situation. In a very basic sense, pain is like a death to an entity; it should be avoided with all its might possible.

RULE 13: All movement is away from pain.

Neera asked me, "Papa, I seem to get an idea about the pain or death and their relation to each other. But since we are talking about general behavior found in every possible kind of organism in this universe, what can we definitely say about a pain or a death?"

I asked, "Let's start with our usual approach. Do you want to refer a dictionary?"

Neera smiled. It seems she had known that I was going to say that. She opened the dictionary page in her mobile phone, which gave the following description of the word *pain*.

pain

noun
- physical suffering or distress
- a distressing sensation in a particular part of the body
- mental or emotional suffering or torment

I asked her, "Are we anywhere close to understand pain by this definition?"

Neera replied, "I don't think so. It says that a pain is a suffering or distress. The question still remains what is a pain, suffering or a distress. Do you want me to look at the word distress?"

I said, "No. It won't help. All it's going to say is that a distress is a pain, anxiety, sorrow, or a suffering. It is like we had figured out last; *a definition of something won't help us know about the thing*. What you have asked is something very fundamental to all life. You want to know what is it that is perceived as a pain, sorrow or suffering by every living creature in this universe."

Neera said, "Exactly! Once again the dictionary doesn't help us in becoming wiser at all! Can we directly jump in and try to figure out what is it that we call as pain or suffering?"

I said, "Why not! Let's see. Let's assume you have a pen that you like very much and don't want to lose it."

Neera said, "Ok".

I asked her, "What do you feel when it is lost or stolen?"

Neera said, "I feel sad."

I asked her, "Can we say that it is a suffering?"

Neera said, "Yes, this is a suffering. Losing something that you don't want to lose is a suffering."

I asked her, "Is losing always a suffering?"

Neera said, "I am not sure that is true. I think one doesn't mind losing something that one doesn't like or need."

I asked, "So, what is the general rule emerging here?"

Neera said, "You like or need some things and don't like or need some other things. You don't want to lose what you have and like it or need it. You want to lose what you have and don't like or need. You want to get something you like or need but don't have. You don't want to get something you don't have but don't like it or need it. How could we state all of that simply?"

I said, "Let's think. We want closeness with things we like. We want distance with things we don't like. Any action opposite to that is painful."

Neera asked, "Are you sure it covers everything and not just humans? Isn't pain mostly a physical thing for all other species?"

I said, "Yes, humans tend to associate a mental association to pain also, which is unique among all other species. For everything else, a pain is a physical experience. Ideally, the body of a living organism is totally complete. When we say that a body is complete, it means that it contains everything it needs. If it loses any part that is needed for its functioning, it feels pain. There are some things that the body needs such as oxygen, water or food. Not getting what you need is painful. There are some thing that the body needs to lose such as toxins and waste matter. Not being able to lose what you don't need is painful too."

Neera said, "It makes perfect sense. Not getting what you need is painful. Getting what you don't need is painful too. Losing what you need is painful. Not losing what you don't need is painful too."

I said, "When we take this rule to its extreme, a pain is like death when what you need is as essential as life itself."

I saw that Neera was satisfied for having brought some clarity on what can be called as a pain or a death. It was about time to move on with our discussion about which movements grab one's attention more than other.

I said, "Let's bring some color into the observation of movement. So far we have talked about size, clarity and prominence of objects in terms of weight or boldness, brightness, contrast or highlighting. We have not talked about color which takes precedence over everything else we have talked so far. Do you believe that a colored section will get an initial attention over everything not so much colored?"

Neera said, "I have never thought about these things ever in my life. But as you are progressively showing me the basic behavioral patterns existing in the observation of movement, I don't disbelieve you. Things seem to be happening quite the same way as you have been showing. I can imagine if there is a plain white statue of Venus with a single red rose in its hair, at first all attention will go to the flower and later to any other part of the statue."

I said, "So true. Here is one such picture here which do show that the attention gets fixated on the colored section in a scene of otherwise not so colorful images. You might have come across many such photographs where only those areas are left colored which need to be looked at by the viewers."

Picture: 6.4 A colored element gets attention in a colorless scene

Picture: 6.5 Mind's attention immediately catches colors out of all colorless elements in a picture

I saw Neera adding one more index card on the top of other three that she had prepared.

Neera asked, "Do we mean to say that size, boldness or contrast doesn't matter if there is something colorful is present in the field of observation?"

I said, "Everything matters as we said, but in the order of precedence. We do notice color, followed by bold contrasting highlighted sections followed by bigger differentiations. For example, in the following picture, the colored word POSITIVE catches attention immediately even though it is quite small in size, as do the words MEMORY in bold and THINK and WORD in color. As soon as the attention has settled on these four, the word BIRTHDAY being the biggest catches attention due to its biggest size. The rest of the words next in size such as ANNIVERSARY, CELEBRATION, HAPPY, LIFE and HOLIDAY are seen in random sequence. If someone continues to pay attention, the next set of words will continue to be noticed in the same sequence of observation.

Picture: 6.6 Mind's prioritized attention to various highlights

Neera asked me, "I have a doubt about all this".

I asked her, "Tell me what your doubt is."

Neera said, "So far we have simplified the whole situation. We took a case where there was just one biggest object, or a few sharp characters, or a little section highlighted through use of color and boldness. I can understand that these ground rules work well in such simplified situations. I am not sure how a complex everyday scenario would be observed with multitude of sights, sounds, variations and colors all around?"

I said, "You have raised a very valid question. We have been talking about the ground rules which influence what movements are observed. When we are discussing the ground rule, we have to take a simple case so that we can understand the principle completely. You have a doubt what happens when in a scene there are many occurrences of equally large objects among everything that is not so large. You may also be confused how a document will be seen with multiple bold sub-titles of same size. You are not sure which one of those movements will be given attention at first."

Neera said, "Yes, this is exactly my confusion".

I asked, "Do you remember our example of clarity?"

Neera said, "Yes, it was a page with many different sized blurry letters, but the attention picked the sharp image of V,O,T and E."

I said, "So the attention went equally to all those characters which were sharper among everything not so sharp and clear."

Neera said, "Yes, The attention didn't pick any particular letter out of the four clear images. You mean to say, our simplified principle works just the same way in all complex situations? If a scene has a few pockets of equally highlighted sections, all will be given the attention at once?"

I said, "Yes, the attention is paid, at once, to all movements which are found similar."

Neera seemed surprised, "I cannot believe it! Do you have any example to convince me about this?"

I said, "As I said, this is a whole different topic that we can discuss about how a complex situation is observed, understood and stored in memory to affect another observation in future. But to satisfy you now, I can show you a couple of examples about how multiple movements are registered at once."

I asked Neera, "Tell me what part in these images makes your attention locked at first when observed?"

Picture: 6.7 All objects with similar qualities get equal attention. All red highlights on windows in first picture get noticed simultaneously, just like all the game pieces in the second picture

Neera said, "When I see the first picture, I notice all the red windows at once. It is just like the rule you mentioned where color takes precedence to everything else such as boldness, clarity or size of objects."

I said, "Correct. There are big cycles taking up almost half of the total picture, yet the attention gets locked on the little windows on the building so far away. There are about fifteen window highlights colored in red, and all are seen at once."

Neera said, "In the other picture there are so many colored game pieces, but I saw all at once as highlighted against the colorless background of the game board. I didn't notice any one single piece in particular at first."

I asked Neera, "So you don't doubt our simple rule which describes observation picks up movements according to some pre-existing principle."

Neera said, "Yes, I think the rule of precedence works the same way whether there is one unique movement or plenty of similar movements. But what if some creature in this universe doesn't have very good eye sight? How do any living being experience these rules of observation, if one doesn't have an ability to identify colors?"

I said, "The rule is being observed by us, the humans, who seem to have the biggest set of senses. It is quite possible that some creatures won't have an ability to see colors. In that case, their order of precedence will still be same, but without colors. They should still experience bolder images, sounds, smells or sensory perceptions taking precedence to sharper perceptions and sharper images taking precedence to bigger perceptions."

Neera said, "It makes sense. So we are saying that observation does not just mean seeing. Observation can be using any one or multiple senses such as seeing, hearing, smelling, touching or tasting. A worm might not be able to see enough, but might be having a great sense of touch or smell to figure out its appropriate actions based on its observations."

"Rightly said." I replied.

"Do you want to move ahead and see what takes precedence to colors when it comes to observation of movements?" I asked Neera.

Neera said, "Let me guess. Is it movement?"

I said, "Yes. Let's call it *animation* or *change* as opposed to a movement. We don't want to confuse ourselves by using the same word meaning two different things. We have already used the word *movement* from the beginning in a very specific sense. When we say animation, we are referring a physical movement or some change in an object's appearance in space or time."

Neera said, "Wow, it was a random guess. Actually I had turned my face towards the kitchen to see what mom was doing there that I *noticed* the digital clock on the microwave blinking. It might have reset due to that power outage that happened yesterday."

I said, "You have been paying attention. So far we have been looking at stationary images and object. The animated movement or a change steals the attention out of everything else we have discussed so far. The microwave clock is so far and its clock digits are hardly readable. There are a few brighter light sources in the direction you looked such as the display panel of the oven, refrigerator, and the bright flood light on the ceiling. Yet, the attention got stuck at the microwave clock because of its blinking. The moment you will set the clock time and its blinking stops, it will stop catching your attention."

Neera said, "I can guess why it makes sense. On a computer screen, our attention will get locked on some particular section depending on color, boldness, clarity or size, but the moment we move the mouse, our eyes start following the curser. The movement of a cursor gets the highest attention out of anything else on the screen. Had it not been the case, we would not have been able to operate computers with screens so easily. On the contrary, we would have to try hard to look for the little cursor among hundreds of details on the screen. If that was the case, the computer's operating system would have made the cursor colorful, bold and big to be noticed easily."

I said, "That's right. The same is true for the presentations where the presenter uses a laser pointer to bring the attention of the audience to the desired section on the screen. The movement of the laser pointer gets the immediate attention and everything else is looked at later, once the movement of the pointer stops. Let us look at the real example of how all these source of capturing attention work together in real life. Do you know what happens when we go out on road for driving in a car?"

Neera replied, "We can see and hear all sort of things. We have the road, buildings, fixtures, trees, birds, people, and all sort of traffic to continuously shift our attention while we go on moving."

I said, "Even though you continue to capture new view every moment while driving, you are able to pay attention to the road side signs informing or warning about the traffic rules. Why is that so?"

Neera said, "All those signs have big, bold, prominent symbols and messages. As we said, an attention will easily lock something big, bold and prominent. To reduce the chance of escaping attention, most signs use colors too, especially with hazard warnings."

I said, "Yes. Even with a lot of activities happening on the roadside and around to distract a driver on the road, the road signs are able to draw the required attention at right moments. The use of all the necessary elements such as color, clarity, boldness and size makes it almost certain that that attention gets locked on the signs."

Neera asked, "But we said that the animation precedes all those qualities. Where is animation in those symbols?"

I said, "You keep the most powerful things for most important use. There are moments when the driver has to pay attention to immediately happening and more important things. The changing traffic lights, the blinking side indicators for turning, the appearance of red brake lights on the vehicles in the front, and all such quickly changing signs are more important and the attention will be naturally drawn to them. It would be catastrophic to use road signs with animated signs because they might divert the attention of the drivers from some immediate danger on the road."

I continued, "However, in the situations of most emergency, the use of loud, bright, blinking and colored lights along with the loud animated sound of siren by the emergency vehicles and police cars are able to get the highest attention as they use every possible means which make it impossible for the observation to miss the movement."

Neera was quietly listening. She was realizing that we all had always been experiencing the real life situation in exactly the same way. Our attentions are noticing the movements in such a predictable manner that we all behave as if we are machines. In fact, we are like machines in the sense that we never actually know that we are behaving like machines. Any quick motion and our heads turn to get a glimpse of it. A sudden noise and our whole body responds to it in reaction. However busy one might be in current moment, the police siren or an emergency alarm gets noticed instantly. The sensation of something crawling on the skin or a thorn piercing through it to generate a sudden pain, the sudden sense of smell of a smoke or a tasty food or a breathtaking fragrance, any quick change, animation or a movement is noticed and an immediate response is generated. It happens with every living thing, every time, without fail.

Neera asked, "Is there anything that takes precedence to animated movement?"

I said, "A quicker or faster movement takes precedence to slower animation or change. If there are two lamps blinking, the fast blinking bulb will draw attention. If there are many cars moving on the road, the attention will catch the fastest moving car or a car making quick turns and variations in its path. Your eyes won't miss the movement of a butterfly, or bird among plants shaking slowing in wind."

Neera asked, "When there is an animated, blinking, shaking or vibrating object, will everything else being highlighted, colored or contrasted become less important?"

I said, "If two objects are animated similarly or changing in the similar fashion, then where the attention falls depends on what comes next in the line of precedence. A colored blinking object will draw focus to the similar blinking object without color, and so on."

Neera said, "I understand. The whole sequence of precedence seems to work such that if two objects are having the similar weightage on some quality, then the next quality in line will decide the center of attention."

I said, "If something is animated and colored, it becomes the easiest center of attention. All business advertisers desire to draw people's attention towards their products. Many times they are able to employ such techniques which use colored objects with animation. The flags and balloons are bright colored and naturally animated in presence of wind. The inflatables use a blower fan to make them create an impression of huge animated characters moving funnily. They make great and cheap advertising gadgets for anyone interested in catching people's attention."

Picture: 6.8 A Mind's attention is bound to catch the prominent, striking, colorful and animated displays

I saw that Neera had prepared two more index cards. The stack looked like this.

Picture: 6.9 Ground Rules of Observation

Neera seemed doubtful. She asked, "I am not still sure why this rule would be the same for every little thing in the universe? Why not any other way?"

I said, "The rule is that attention goes first towards faster movements, then slower movements, then color, contrast, highlights, clarity and then finally to size. Let us picture a scenario in which some living entity observes a few things. Which one will it be interested in immediately?"

Neera said, "I don't know."

I asked, "What were our life rules?"

Neera guessed, "*All movement is away from pain* (Rule: 13). Every movement is towards safety?"

I asked, "And what does it mean when something seems or sounds big? Is it not possible that the object is nearer than other things not so big?"

Neera said, "Yes, when something looks big or sounds loud or smells stronger, it is probable it is nearer."

I asked, "If it is about safety, which thing should the attention go to?"

Neera said, "The bigger one, or the louder one".

I asked, "If it is about survival and elimination of hunger, which thing should the attention go to?"

Neera said, "Again, the bigger one, as it might be closer."

I said, "So whether it is about running away from or running towards, the bigger one must get the attention as it might be more immediate than any other object in observation."

Neera asked, "That makes sense. What about clarity?"

I asked, "If there is a big thing but it is blurry. There is another thing but sharp and focused. Which of these has more chances of being closer?"

Neera said, "The blurrier object has chances of being farther than the sharper one. If I was a mouse, I would be less scared of large blurry ball than a tiny sharp image of a spider."

I asked, "If there is a blurry object, a sharp object and a slowly moving object, which one will a living organism be bothered about?"

Neera said, "The moving one. It is more important whether as a threat or as an opportunity. If a threat, the living being needs to protect itself. If an opportunity, it might be lost as it is moving. All stationary objects have lesser chances of being lost than the currently moving one."

I asked her, "Doesn't life seems to be doing great with itself when it comes to having one set of standard rules for everything?"

Neera said, "It seems so, with the way we are imagining the world. But how does knowing all this make me wiser?"

I said, "When you know how everything and everybody observes, you become wiser. You are wise if you cannot be fooled. For example, if you know that water does not burn, and someone shows lighting a fire in the water, you can guess that a trick is being played. In the same way, when you know what influences the movement of attention in any observation, your wisdom stops you from being deceived by others trying to influence your attention."

Neera said, "I don't get it how someone can try to deceive or influence attention."

I said, "In the world of consumerism, every business is trying to sell its products and services by making it seem appealing to masses. They use all the possible means to bring your attention to what they want to show and away from what they don't want to show, but still have to present to you for legal purposes."

Neera said, "This is strange. I always thought what is legal is always what is right!"

I said, "Yes, what I am saying is quite the opposite. Look at these pictures. The advertisers have used big, bold messages to form a particular (false) impression in the minds of readers. They have mentioned the real message in the form of very tiny letters which can hardly be read even if someone tries to pay attention. You become wise when you know how you are being tried to be cheated and influenced by manipulating your basic instincts of observation of movements."

Picture: 6.10 Advertisers use different sized letters to force the attention at selective information creating bias in customer's minds

In this picture, while in the big print it claimed fastest internet, the package being advertised actually provided the slowest internet to its consumers. The way attention works, a reader gets the following message:

$99.99 -> a month for two years -> Such a small price for a big deal -> amazing picture .. fastest internet ..

The world is increasingly becoming more and more dependent on information. The information is always so large and the time so short that it is highly unlikely that someone will disbelieve what seems obvious and instead go read the smallest message first. Here is yet another example:

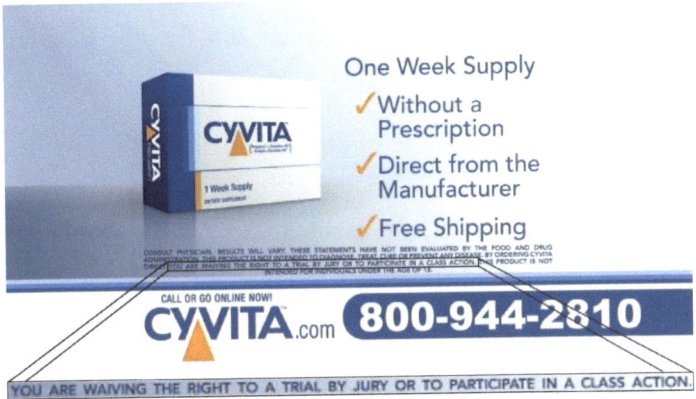

Picture: 6.11 Advertisers use different sized letters to force the attention at selective information creating bias in customer's minds

In this picture, the advertiser has used big and bold words for all that they wish the reader to pay attention to. But for the most important legal issue, they used the smallest letters possible. While they satisfy the legal requirement of bringing all information to the consumers, they have ensured that a consumer would hardly ever notice it.

Wisdom is being able to differentiate what is legal from what is right. People have been educated and trained for many years from the very young age to become someone who is anything but a wise person. People spend their whole life following rules, regulations, laws and instructions; get motivated by petty rewards and continuously scared of punishments, go on complying. They are forced to pay attention to the way that suits to the governments, religious organizations and the powerful corporations. It is rare for someone to be able to pay attention to what is happening around free of conditioning and figure out if what is seen is actually what is.

I was trying to wake up the most intelligent form of all existence, the human being, in the little Neera. I know it was hard, tedious and next to impossible task to wake people who have had a habit of sleeping for millions of years. Neera has not yet grown completely; she hasn't yet been totally *educated* by the society. There is still a little hope, that maybe, I might get her to wake up before the strong spell of social conditioning puts her to a sleep of her lifetime. If that happens, she will be struggling all her remaining life, driven by everything else around her, except for her own conscious and aware mindfulness.

7

Observation with Memory

Neera learns about observation in presence of memory and past experiences which creates a partial & conditioned view of the universe.

Neera asked me, "I can understand that there is a set sequence of how movements capture attention based on how quickly changing, contrasted or big they are. The ground rules of observation may be same for every single entity in this universe, yet each species might behave totally different in similar situations. We talked in the past that some species might not have a developed sense of recognizing colors. Some others might hear the sounds in a totally different spectrum. The movements that such species observe in a scene might be totally different than some other species. Don't you think that the theory you have developed about the universal ground rule seems incomplete?"

I said, "We have noted down the criteria of observation based on our own observations. How we experience observation is a super-set of how everyone else will because we as humans are most advanced in overall use of senses. If in the universe there are species more advanced than humans, there is a possibility that our observations might not cover the universal rule. But as long as we have not known anything more developed than humans, we will assume this rule covers all observation in the universe as we know it. As we mentioned, the sequence of priority of observation of movements is valid all the time for all the observations. All those who do not have senses to capture a particular kind of feature ignore those kinds of movements, but the remaining sensory perception still follows the same priority. In summary, the observation of movement happens in this sequence.

> **Priority of Observation of Movements (through senses such as seeing, hearing, smelling, touching or tasting):**
> - *Fastest animations* (quick changes, blinking, ringing, moving, swinging) are recognized fist, followed by:
> - *Slower animations* followed by
> - *Colors* followed by
> - *High contrasts* (brightness, boldness, differentiation) followed by
> - *Sharp and clearer images* followed by
> - *Bigger and larger objects* (shapes, images, sounds, feelings).

Neera asked, "What you are saying is not how everything works in this world. Each human sees and interprets in his own way and acts based on those faulty interpretations to create conflicts everywhere. Why should anyone believe that every observation is exactly predictable as you mentioned."

I said, "We have talked about the universal ground rules of observation. This is how every little entity or a whole group of entities experiences movement. The difference in one human from other is not in the way they observe the movements. The two humans observe two totally different movements in a same situation because they might notice and interpret the qualities such as the size, contrast, colors in light of their past experiences, education, culture, habits. Every person goes on collecting various experiences during his (or her) lifetime and keeps them stored in the memory. The memory of past experiences affects how future observations are made. So far we have talked about observation without reference of any past memory."

Neera asked, "I can see that in case of most of the animals, birds, insects and other creatures the experience of observation might not involve past memory. But do humans ever experience observation of movement without past memory, experience or habit?"

I said, "Why not? It is the education, learning and experience that affect the quality of observation. Children are experiencing observation devoid of much memory or conditioning because they haven't had much experience of past remembrances. All humans too, when facing huge conflicts, crisis or emergency situations experience observation free of conditioning."

Neera asked, "Is that so? Is there any example where all humans act in the same way?"

I said, "If you see an office building, every person going in or coming out of it is unique in the manner of walking, talking and behaving. However, when there is a fire in a building, everybody will be running around trying to save himself or herself. No two people will be acting different from each other. A fire is the highest form of crisis and in such a situation everyone will do what is most important, the safety of oneself or one's loved ones."

Neera asked, "And you mentioned children. Do all children behave similarly in a situation?"

I said, "Have you heard of a story about some television show being shared on social media, where a toddler is offered to choose between some toys and a check worth one million dollars? Every toddler picks the toys while its helpless parents watch it from far. The story might not be true but it predicts the behavior of toddlers rightly because a colored piece of object gathers more attention than a little piece of paper from the point of observation of the toddler."

Neera asked, "You used the word conditioning when talking about observing with memory. Why is an observation with memory a conditioned observation? What is wrong with a conditioned observation?"

I said, "Every kind of learning conditions our behavior to prepare ourselves for future. If you have been hurt by the thorns of a particular bush a few times, you remember the pain and learn to avoid the plant in future. Your experience and memory of the pain makes you avoid all similar plants found anywhere else. *The memory of pain conditions your observation.* It is a survival mechanism for all living beings. In any future observation, this plant becomes one bold, contrasted entity and gets noticed immediately in your observations. What becomes a prominent object in your observation might not be even noticed by another person who never had a bad experience with this plant. Humans have a highly developed brain and a huge capacity to memorize. The basic survival instinct combined with high memory continues to shape their future observations in a highly conditioned manner."

Neera asked, "This looks like a complex situation. How can I understand observation in presence of memory in easy manner?"

I said, "I can try to make it easier. Now that we have discussed what observation, frame of reference and movement are, we can find out how a memory affects how movements are observed."

Neera said, "Before we start talking about observing with memory, let me read all that I have written in my notebook about (plain) observation." Then she started reading the important points one by one.

Nature of Observation:
- Frame of Reference or Observer is the point of observation
- Frame of Reference or Observer is non-moving
- To observe is to know
- There is no observation in absence of movement; there is no knowing in absence of movement;
- Only changes are noticed; knowledge is relative
- The necessary condition for a movement to exist is the knowledge of movement in space and time from a point of reference, the observer

I said, "That should give us a good point to start. We shall start our journey from the beginning of time."

Neera said, "I don't know what you mean by beginning of time."

I said, "Beginning of time is that place before which nothing existed."

Neera asked, "How do we go to a place before which nothing existed?"

I said, "When you start observing without using any existing memory, knowledge or past experience, you are at the beginning of time."

Neera said, "I don't think that is true. Even if it was true, it won't be easy as we are so much used to working with our memory".

I said, "Don't worry about this being difficult. We both will watch each other to help avoid our memories to interrupt our investigation."

Neera asked, "I am ready. What do we do now that we are at the beginning of time?"

I said, "We don't do anything. We just remain observant."

Neera was quiet. It seems she already knew what being observant meant. She had seen me many times, sitting quietly doing nothing. She was there on the carpet comfortably seated by support of a cushion. We were not speaking, yet the room was filled with various sounds. The ceiling fan, the refrigerator in the kitchen, the pool motor and air-conditioner unit operating in the backyard, and the continuous chirping of different birds outside our house; everything was going on as usual. It seems, our sitting quietly didn't stop the working of the universe in any way.

I pushed a blank paper in front of Neera. She looked at it quickly and then looked at me raising her eyebrows. I didn't say anything. She could not help it, and asked me, "What about it?"

I asked her, "What do you see?"

Neera said, "It's a blank paper."

I asked, "I have shown you a paper. What do you see on the paper?

Neera said, "Absolutely nothing. It's simply blank."

I asked, "Can you continue looking at the paper?"

Neera said, "No. Unless there is something drawn or made out on paper that can get my attention, I cannot continue looking. The paper is like a big background on which the attention seeks some form of a movement. There is nothing to know in absence of a movement. If there is nothing to know, there is a strong sense of boredom, tiredness, restlessness."

I said, "You named the paper as background. You said there is absolutely nothing contrasted, or any sort of movement which stands out against the background to allow drawing the attention. Do you mean to say that there is absolutely no movement which could be observed from the paper as the frame of reference or point of observation?"

Neera said, "This is right. If there were any drawing, coloring, perforations, objects or embossing on the paper, the condition for movement might exist from the point of view of the paper as being the frame of reference or an observer."

I asked, "Look at the paper. Is there any movement? Is there any noticing?"

Neera said, "No."

I asked, "What did we say about a situation when there is no movement?"

Neera said, "That *there is no observer in absence of a movement.*"

I said, "True, The blank paper is similar to a situation of no observer and no movement. There is nothing happening, nowhere. There is no time, space, observer or observation."

Neera said, "The beginning of time!"

I smiled. It *was* the beginning of time. We had no knowledge, no memory, no expectation, no idea what comes next. We were not hopeful. We were not frustrated. These all emotions exist only in time, when we have an idea about our existence. In the beginning of time, there are no ideas, no existence, and no future.

I took the paper and drew a little mouse quickly.

Neera said, "Now, there I see a little something in the corner!"

I was smiling. She had really gone in the beginning of time where she had no concept of naming something. I said, "Let's start calling it a mouse. Let's discuss what has happened here."

Neera said, "On the background, the observer or the frame of reference, there was an appearance of some new pattern. We already mentioned in the past that *only changes are observed*. We may call this change as birth of something. In other words, a change is observed as a birth of a pattern. We identify it as a mouse. The background or the frame of reference was empty or blank paper which was devoid of anything worth noticing."

I said, "So you have mentioned two important parts of an observation, the movement and the background. You could also call them as the observer and the observed. Can you name the two distinct elements of the observation in case of this paper?"

Neera said, "The observed is the little mouse in the corner. The observer is the background."

I said, "We can see that there are two distinct elements in the observation. The mouse and everything not mouse. Do you recall something like this we encountered in the past?"

Neera said, "Yes, the color paper experiment where we asked people to color every part of paper that was not-apple."

I said, "Likewise, on this paper too, there is a mouse, and then there is no-mouse everywhere else. You called the mouse as the observed because it is the center of attention. It became the center of attention as the most recent change that happened on the background (the paper). The rest of the paper (the not-mouse) is the background, the frame of reference, or the point of observation or simply, the observer."

Neera said, "I love it; it's so different than the way I normally looked at anything before! There is no Neera in this whole observation thing. There is only a background (the observer), and the movement (the observed)."

I probed further, "Is the background something totally empty and devoid of anything or it is something where the attention does not go; cannot go?"

Neera said, "Are these not two different things; the background being empty versus it containing something that cannot be seen? If I can't see in the store room because it is dark in there, it doesn't mean that it is empty."

I asked, "Is it not something that we have already gone over? The store room is dark and you cannot figure out if there is anything in there. Since there is no movement, there is no appropriate action. Do you remember the rules we established already? We said that if something has not been observed, it doesn't exist (*In absence of observation, there is no movement*)."

Neera said, "Oh, I remember! It is such a radical thought that I haven't yet absorbed it completely. I can see that you asked me if the background is really empty or that there is nothing worth seeing. These two are really the same thing if we can appreciate that a thing does not exist (for us) if not known (by us). If there is nothing worth seeing or noticing in the background, the attention does not get there; cannot go there. If the attention does not notice anything, then nothing exists. So, how do I answer it? It does not matter if the background is empty or not. All it matters is that it cannot be observed. It cannot be observed because the observer *is the background*."

I asked, "So what do we say about the paper?"

Neera asked back, "What? Haven't we said it already? What else do we say about it?"

"Is that all? Are we done looking at the paper, discussing about it?" I asked.

Neera said, "Yes. What else do we see here? There was a blank paper. Then there appeared a mouse. And now it's been quite some time that nothing has happened. It's a paper with a mouse on its corner."

She had a glance at the paper while she was speaking. She was right. There was nothing else to talk about. What was there to observe? *It was just a paper with a mouse in one of the corners!*

There is absolutely no movement. There is nothing worth paying attention to. *A change is all that is noticed.* There is nothing changing in this picture. *It's just a little mouse in the corner.*

Initially the background was an empty paper with nothing over it. In a matter of time, the background is being known as a paper with a mouse in the corner. There is nothing worth noticing. It is boring to look at. If things don't change, the attention will never capture the mouse. Within a short span of time, the non-moving mouse has become the background. Everything worth knowing about the mouse has been known. *Knowledge is memory. Knowledge is conditioning.* The knowledge of the past memories and experiences creates a background of our conditioning. The conditioned background is the observer whose point of view defines the nature of observation. A drunken person's observation will not be the same as a person who is not drunk. When he comes to his senses, the drunken person will not be able to observe what was observed while in state of drunkenness. The movement noticed depends on the observer. Observer defines the observed. *Observer is the observed.*

The current view had settled in our minds. The paper was not empty like before, yet was devoid of any (further) knowledge. It was no more a blank paper with a picture of mouse. It was a paper with a picture of mouse. I took the sheet of paper and drew another thing quickly.

Neera exclaimed, "Ah! I see something."

Movement is the nature of life. Movements are the only things that will be noticed. *Non-movement is death*; it's opposite of life, the movement. *A death is when the attention is not*, because movement means attention.

The life is the continuity of attention on movement; death is the end of noticing of movement. They both are happening at the same time; all the time.

The blank paper was filled with life when a little mouse

appeared in a corner. Before its appearance, there was no life (on paper). The attention lasted momentarily with the new change, but soon enough knowledge was acquired about the change. The acquired knowledge became part of memory and learning. That which was noticed as a movement merged into the background in a matter of time. A new change was needed or else all the non-movement was again like a death. *All movement is life.* The attention cannot remain on the dead background. It has to land on another movement happening somewhere else. Everything in the universe is continuously moving, changing shapes and arrangement. Being fixated on one thing that is permanent, non-changing is boredom, painful and is like death. There is no end to finding a movement to notice. It is always happening. The life is the continuity of attention on movement; death is the end of noticing of movement. They both are happening at the same time; all the time.

Neera asked, "But things don't just continue to add up in our observation. Thing go out of observation too. How does this thing work if one or more things get away from the field of observation? What if I ease one mouse on the paper?"

I said, "Getting out of the field of observation is a movement too. It is a change, therefore, It is noticed! Have you not noticed writers using the phrase about someone being *conspicuous by one's absence*? If something has become a routine, its absence will be noticed."

"I get it. But, is that all? Every new movement is observed, ignored or acted upon, registered as learning or experience in memory and again ready for the next movement?" Neera asked.

I said, "That is all! This is the whole cycle of universal movement. Religious scriptures and wise people call it the cycle of *birth, sustenance and death*."

Neera said, "I don't believe it! Just by looking at the process of observation for a few minutes, we can understand the way whole universe operates!"

I said, "This is true. We can go over any number of examples of such observations. You will find that the attention (to a movement) is momentary. As soon as a change is observed, it is registered, evaluated, processed and therefore becomes *known*. *Once known, a change ceases to be a change*."

Neera said, "You said you would talk about observation in presence of memory. But we haven't yet talked about it."

I said, "Haven't we? At first you had a blank paper. Remember, we were at the beginning of time, with no memory, experience or any remembrance. Then came a mouse from somewhere. Within no time the mouse became a part of memory, a part of the background for further movement. The appearance of mouse and its recognition as a part of observation soon became the memory, the knowledge. This knowledge was the new background, on which the further movements were registered, such as another mouse."

I continued, "What we observe in our everyday life is from the frame of reference, a background built over our lifetime from memories of our experiences and our habits. Since every human has experienced life uniquely, no two people can look at any situation in the same way. An observer is nothing but the background, and the background is nothing but the collection of past observations stored as memory. *We see what we are.*"

"I can now understand what it means when we say what we are is what we see. Perhaps, more than a tongue twister", Neera added some humor.

I was waiting for Neera to ask another question. I had explained her how our everyday observations continue to add to our memory as learning and knowledge. Having known that

> **Having known that the huge load of memories and experiences collected over our lifetime build a background from where the new observations are seen, it leaves hardly any room for much observation as we grow old.**

the huge load of memories and experiences collected over our lifetime build a background from where the new observations are seen, it leaves hardly any room for much observation as we grow old. We become a heavy load of old memories and experiences having known and seen almost everything in this world. Nothing can make us interested or excited as almost everything going on around us has already been known. In a way, if existing knowledge is the deterrent for new knowledge, what is the way out? I was hoping Neera too was pondering over this.

"Am I just a bag of old memories?" Neera asked.

I said, "*You are what you see*. What you see is what you already are. If you carry the load of your past experiences and view the world from such a background, you are nothing but a dead entity. You are never going to look at the world with fresh eyes as long as you remain conditioned."

Neera asked, "Is the memory and experience the only conditioning? Is there anything else?"

I said, "The ideas we collect as a part of our culture, nationality, religion and relations; all of these create conditioning in humans. They create a huge bag of *known*."

"But how do you not see anything with the eyes of the known? Don't I recognize a mango, the moment I see one in the grocery store? What is the advantage of not using memory?" Neera asked.

I said, "Memory and experience is the greatest gift we have as humans. It makes us make smart and intelligent decisions in carrying ourselves through the life. Just like a knife is a wonderful tool when used in kitchen when needed and not for carrying with us all the time, we should use memory only when needed."

Neera said, "So what you are saying is that memory, knowledge and experience are both useful as well as dangerous!"

I said, "Yes, and the wisdom is to give them their right place, use it when needed, and shut them off when not needed."

Neera said, "And how does one know when to use it or when to shut them off. Moreover, it isn't easy to shut the memory off. What you remember is always in your mind. If I hate someone, I carry it with me all the time and use it any time I happen to come close to that person or even think about him or her. It is nearly impossible to use my memory and experience as I want. *I am my memory and experience*; not someone different than that."

> "I am my memory and experience; not someone different than that."

I said, "Rightly said, *you are that*; you are a bundle of all your memories and experiences. This is another one of the brilliant messages by Mr. Jiddu Krishnamurty".

Neera asked, "How do we get command over this conditioning? How do we become master of ourselves?"

I said, "You will gain mastery if you strongly desire for this. We will talk about this some other time."

8

Present Moment is the key

Every life decision is influenced by the forces of pain and pleasure in the present moment

"We talked in the past about the life rules. Do you remember what those were?" I asked Neera.

Neera said, "I remember them. We said every living being treats pain the same was as it treats the death. Every movement is away from pain, or death."

I said, "Right. And since the opposite of death is life, and that of pain is pleasure or happiness, you could also say that *every movement is towards pleasure, happiness or life.*"

Neera said, "That seems logical."

I said, "Though it seems logical, the force of repulsion from pain or death is far stronger than the force of attraction to life or pleasure."

Neera was confused, "I don't understand."

I said, "If a pleasure is only available at the cost of facing pain, the pleasure has to be much higher than the pain."

Neera asked, "I might understand what you are saying, but I cannot visualize it. Can you please explain it with an example?"

I said, "If you see a one dollar bill stuck deep in a thorny bush, there is a good chance that you would not want to undergo painful process to get it. But if it happens to be a $100 bill, you will be willing to put yourself to some pain and discomfort, because the reward outweighs the pain."

Neera said, "Oh, I see!"

I said, "This simple rule (action dependent on two opposite forces – reward and punishment) seems to be the central force governing all movements in the universe. In this sense, humans are no different than any other creature in the world. Our everyday behavior is being guided by the two opposite forces, the rewards and the punishments. We continue to run in different directions based on our own interpretation of pleasures and pains."

Neera asked, "Is there nothing that we do which is not an outcome of these forces?"

I asked her back, "Is there? You tell me. What happens when a person is asked to do something?"

Neera said, "If someone asks me to do something, I ask for the reason, purpose or the need."

I asked, "What do we mean when we want to know the purpose of something? Are we not trying to figure out what good is it to do the task? Conversely does it not mean what bad is it trying to avoid? Is it not a question about finding the nature of force whether it's about achieving a reward or avoiding a punishment?

Neera said, "I find it interesting. I never thought every little movement has got to be either about wanting to get something or wanting to avoid something. Is this life just such a little piece of programming in all of the living beings?"

I said, "Well, this is what it seems. Everyone avoids pain and prefers pleasure."

Neera added, "And Pain is far stronger than Pleasure!"

I said, "Rightly said. Let's revisit our model for observation and action. We had used a comparator to explain how a movement is sensed and a corresponding action is initiated. Now we are saying that the corresponding action is actually dependent on the kind of movement registered. The direction and intensity of action is dependent on the nature of movement; it is towards the movement if for pleasure and life oriented and away from movement if it is painful or life threatening."

I went ahead and updated the model we made so far.

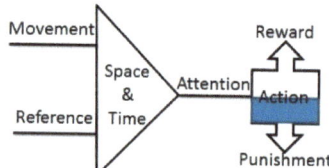

Picture: 8.1 Observation-Action Pair

Neera said, "Let me understand the basic life rules we mentioned so far." She then wrote down the following rules:

- All movement is away from death
- Pain is like death
- All movement is away from pain
- All movement is toward pleasure or happiness
- Pain is far more stronger than pleasure

I thought it was a good idea for her to list down what we had already gone over so far. She had written down the main idea, but it was still very confusing how an action gets done in presence of conflicting forces, life as well as death. How do different living beings decide whether to go towards pleasure or run away from the danger, when both are present?

If I am faced with a death like situation, do I care to fulfil my hunger more than avoiding death? Do I not have it programmed in myself an idea that the death is the most important things to avoid, even if it is at the cost of remaining hungry, painful, less happy? Or maybe, this is exactly what is programmed in every living being in this universe. Assuming that all organisms have this idea of saving themselves from pain, torture or death, how do they prioritize the urgency in terms of time? Some of the organisms are so primitive that they hardly have any sense of rationalizing, prioritizing or delaying decisions. Yet, each one has an instinct for survival. Every creature tries to avoid its death. The only rule that works for every creature is that the decision is made in the very moment a movement is noticed. This was in line with our earlier discussion that all the *actions (as a result of noticing a movement) are immediate.*

In view of considering every possible kind of creatures in the universe, there can be only one ground principle in presence of conflicting movements.

RULE 14: All effort is towards avoiding death in the present moment.

Conversely, if there is no death in the present moment, what would a simple creature do? Does it have any idea about future? Can it imagine a future risk of a present moment? A future event is something non-existent for a simple mind. If there is no death in the moment, then it simply doesn't exist. The only driving force will be the possible gain or pleasure in the current moment.

RULE 15: The (idea of) death doesn't matter if it is not in the present moment.

I told Neera that we could go over a few real life examples and see if this is really the rule that works everywhere and with everyone. She willingly agreed and started thinking of some scenarios. I too got up to make myself a hot cup of tea while pondering over different situations that could be faced by all sorts of creatures facing life and death. As I started measuring the right mix of water and milk to put to boil in the pot, my thoughts kept racing. I visualized many situations such as waking up, getting ready for work, facing various challenges in office, driving on the road, spending time on weekend and so on. It somehow, didn't seem to work. There was not really a serious conflict or a life and death situation. Then I thought of some different kinds of movies involving crime, murder, jealousy, mystery and continued to think of some situations while adding sugar and tea to the boiling mix. In about ten minutes, my tea was ready but mind was still blank and without any real examples.

Then it suddenly happened! I was reminded of something that bothered me for a long time. It was about the human behavior that I found unexplainable in so many situations. It was their indifference to various warnings or threats they received in different forms at different times. It was the difference between what they said and how they behaved. It was the contradiction between their beliefs and their actions. It was as if you would never know whether people were really dumb or they were simply following how the nature had made them to be. It was unexplainable because I used to think humans as different from all other creatures in having a logical mind. It seemed what looked to me as a human stupidity or sluggishness to respond to most situations in a logical way, was really the way nature had designed every living being.

It seems that I came to know now why were humans behaving irrationally. It was all about making decision in the present moment, the ground rule that applies to each and every living creature in this universe. All that each living being cares in the moment is the pain or death in the moment, not in the future. No doubt people do not pay attention to a warning about future danger whether it is about increasing toxicity in the rivers, oceans and underground water or it is about reducing natural resources such as water, oil and food. As long as the danger is not now, it is not an issue. One in every ten, twenty or a few hundred people might use discretion or think rationally, but we are talking about the majority of humans making decision in a busy world.

For all my life, I saw warnings displayed on the packets of cigarettes about its harmful effects. I saw the people being told in every possible way about the health risks of smoking. Every person on the earth knows it well that smoking might result in earlier and painful death. Contrary to what one would expect, none of such warnings has ever stopped anyone to quit smoking habit out of the fear of a future discomfort. Why? Because this is how all living beings are programmed. Not choosing to smoke is painful in the present moment; it like a death. The harmful effects of smoking might kill in the future, but letting go the opportunity of pleasure in the present moment by skipping smoking is a pain; like a death in the present moment. As we figured out the rule of life, a movement in the present moment is always in the direction to avoid death in this moment. *No warning will ever stop people from doing what they want to do.*

I was glad that things were fitting perfectly. The humans were not different than anything else in the universe. What a little creature would have done a million years ago is what a human being will do a million years later; a movement towards survival; a movement away from death. There is no concept of time when decisions are made for action emerging out of an observation. The observation, decision making and action are all one integrated act happening in a timeless manner. I spent next few minutes revealing to Neera what I had figured out about the life rule and its application in the present moment. She listened silently and with great interest and seemed to relate to her own understanding of the world.

She asked me, "Doesn't finding the root cause of a problem give us a clue to solve it too?"

I said, "That is right. If you know the root cause of a problem, you already know how to solve it.

> **There is no concept of time when decisions are made for action emerging out of an observation. The observation, decision making and action are all one integrated act happening in a timeless manner.**

Observation is action. If you have observed it completely, the action is bound to be there."

I remembered something that I saw recently in my office. I told Neera about a message that the Human Resource department posted near the elevator. The three storied office building houses about a thousand employees but has only one elevator. In order to discourage the use of elevator, and motivate people to use stairs, they posted the following message near the elevator. I asked Neera if she thought this could make any significant impact on people's behavior.

Picture: 8.2 Warnings or Messages can't drive an Action

Neera saw the poster that mentioned benefits of using stairs. It was clearly the kind of situation she had asked me about a few minutes back. Neera said, "If I intended to take an elevator and find this poster when I was about to board it, I wouldn't easily change my mind and take stairs just because someone reminded me about the long term benefits. I might be too tired at the moment to think about my long term benefits. As you mentioned, *it is all about the pain and suffering in the moment that decides the actions* that I take in that moment."

I asked Neera, "Can you think laterally and come out with an idea that would make a difference; something that can make people to choose stairs than to use the elevator?"

Neera said, "I am sure it must be something scary, or something that makes this journey painful. Some information about the elevator being risky might scare people off, but might not be legal to do so. They could use some other techniques which could discourage people from using it. The elevator could be made extremely slow or very noisy, or very uncomfortable so as to frustrate the people who, then slowly change over to other alternative, the stairs."

I said, "Yes, everything you said is right. A motivating message does not largely drive people to do something. Even if it does, it does not have the intensity, the same power that a negative or a painful experience has. The will to live and avoid the pain is far stronger to the mind than a will to get a little more comfortable."

She said, "I would guess that if we really wanted people to quit smoking, we would have understood the uselessness of such messages long time ago. We would have tried some means that actually worked and motivated or forced people away from the habit of smoking."

I said, "Yes, if this was really what we wanted to do. We would not use a futuristic idea of death, but would inflict pain in the present moment to force people to avoid smoking."

Neera said, "One way to make it seem painful could be by making cigarettes extremely expensive. If I were to pay $100 for a pack of cigarettes, I would better not smoke."

I said, "That might do it! Make them realize pain or death in the present moment. The mind will process all available rewards and punishments in the present moment before making any decision about an action. It cannot work on different things in different time. It is not equipped to do it."

Neera said, "I have a question in my mind. You said that a majority of human beings will make decisions based on their natural instincts, just like anything else in this universe. This is in contrast to what we think of humans who are gifted with a brain to store, analyze and process information. What is that mechanism which makes us all unknowingly behave like programmed machines?"

I said, "It is called, the Mind."

Neera asked, "Is the mind not same as the brain?"

I said, "No. What we refer to as brain is a physical structure with ability to store, analyze and process information. What we call as mind, is the general rule that is universally operating everywhere, all the time in all the places for each one. You may say, the universe is nothing but the mind. If you know how the universe works you have known mind. You could also say that if you have known the (ways of) the mind, you have known the universe. If you have known a thing in its entirety, then you have also known how to act, because *observation (or knowledge) is action.*"

Neera said, "In that case, I would like to know what is the mind so completely that I don't behave like most ignorant humans, living unaware of their own behaviors."

I said, "Sure. Next time, we will try to see how the mind works. Once we have known how it operates, we will already have known how to take control of the mind. But, before we do that, let's make a picture of what we learnt today."

Neera asked, "A picture of the way decisions are made in the present moment?"

I said, "Yes. Would you like to draw a simple picture?"

Neera agreed to do it. I sat there watching her go over her notes and trying to draw and revise the picture. I could have shown her myself, but was making it sure that she started grasping how to understand, think and explain using pictures, something that she needed her mind to learn and create a habit of. She made the following model depicting how decisions are made in presence of alternative choices.

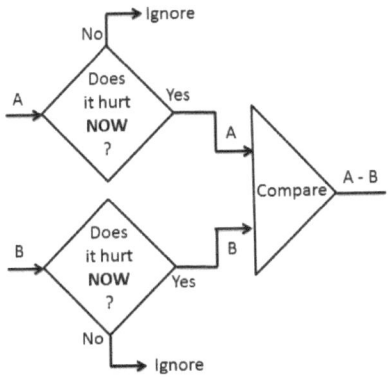

Picture: 8.3 Choice making in presence of conflicting alternatives

I was satisfied with what she had drawn. She made is sure to highlight the word 'now' to emphasize that the ground of all decision making was the present moment. I asked her if she could use the flow chart to explain some real life situations we discussed involving such decision making. She asked me if she could use the same example of dilemma about quitting smoking when exposed with warning statements. I thought that would be a good example to start with, as we had already covered the base. She spent the next fifteen minutes preparing the example on the lines of the choice making flow-chart. It looked like this.

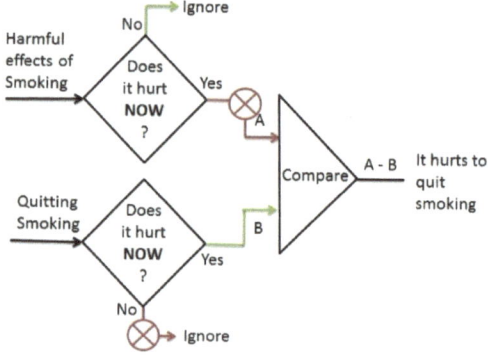

Picture: 8.4 Why a warning about future
does not end a comfort zone

I noticed that she had titled her drawing introducing the word 'comfort zone'. I had not thought about naming the whole process, but now that she named it, it seemed to make perfect sense. It has been noticed and known by everyone that it is painful to come out of one's comfort zone. Yet, instead of understanding the root cause of origination of a comfort zone, people continue to advocate applying discipline, goal, effort and will power to come out of it. Once it is known that the comfort zone is the natural instinct found in all living beings, it can be easily figured out how to force oneself out of it. It is just like someone comfortably sitting on the couch watching television responds immediately by jumping out when a scorpion is sighted. The decisions and actions are taken in the present moment without a second thought. Once the root cause of such actions is known, one wouldn't suggest posting another warning message to stop people. One would innovatively introduce an element of pain in the present moment associated with the choice. Putting exorbitant price on a cigarette is one such act. I asked Neera to draw the effect of introducing the pain of expensive cigarettes on choice making. She did.

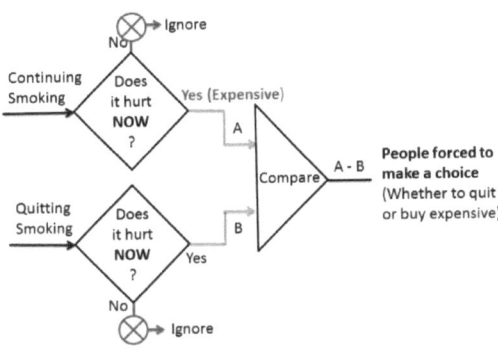

Picture: 8.5 End of comfort zone by introducing pain in the present moment

I told Neera that a real pain isn't necessary in all the cases to create alternative forcing choices, sometimes an idea of pain also works in the same way. Assume that there is a boy who wishes to go for morning jog but feels lazy every morning. At that time in the morning, feeling relaxed in the bed, the idea of getting out and jog is more painful for the boy than the possible advantages of morning jog every day. He has been encouraged many times in the past by various books, friends and relatives, but none of all that motivation has a power to pull him out of bed in the morning. *The motivation to try new things is as useless as a warning to avoid doing something.* They don't have any real existence in the present moment.

I asked Neera, "What do you think works sometimes in such cases? What can pull someone out of the comfort zone?"

Neera said, "From what it seems, we would need to introduce another instance of pain, or an idea of pain as you just suggested."

I said, "This is right. In many school hostels, students are required to wake up early and collect in the PT grounds for morning routine. The school teachers know the painful choice the students need to make in the morning, so they introduce punishments to ensure that all students comply with the norms."

Neera asked, "In this example where the boy is neither in school nor is he in control of anybody who could inflict a pain, what sort of pain would present him an alternative choice?"

I said, "I am sure you would have seen in a few movies where the boy has a crush on his next door neighbor. What do you think he does when he comes to know that the girl goes for an early morning walk?"

Neera said, "He happily jumps out of bed next morning!"

I said, "Yes, there is the idea of pain in that moment, the pain of missing an opportunity to come face to face with his crush."

I asked Neera if she could draw a flow chart of choices in the 'present moment' for him. She did.

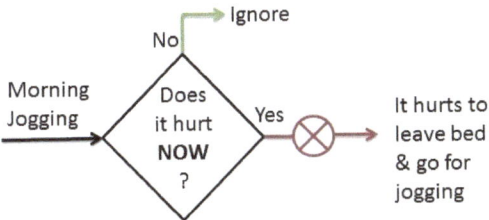

Picture: 8.6 Decision making in comfort zone

She also drew the renewed choices in presence of another idea of pain associated with choice making. She understood that *when it comes to leaving your comfort zone, it is all about the presence of punishment or an idea of a pain in the present moment.*

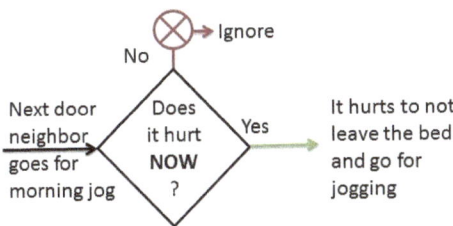

Picture: 8.7 Decision making in comfort zone depends on the idea of pain in present moment

For the next hour we both sat and discussed if this is how humans seemed to act commonly in the world. The behavior always seemed to be driven by the amount of pain in the current moment. The action never depends on what is a proper or improper action; it was always about moving such that the current pain or death is avoided. Neera asked me why our whole decision making was only talking about pain or death. She wondered if the pleasure or happiness could also be the driving factors in the present moment for an action. I explained to her that pain and happiness were just as relative feelings as any other relative measure such as big or small, dark or light, high or low. *I showed her that a pleasure is nothing but a lesser pain.* Initially she found this very strange. But soon after I showed her a few examples, she began to realize the truth in it. You find injections painful. When after a dog bite, you were scared to get fourteen injections in the stomach, and the doctor said that you would need only three injections in the arm, you suddenly feel happy. As the pain reduces, you feel happy. Here were a few situations we thought of, where someone could try to apply the reasoning about dealing with pain in the present moment and see the appropriate action taken by a concerned entity.

1. *A boss has two subordinates Lazia and Wizzy. Lazia is a lazy and insincere and her work quality is inferior. Wizzy is smart, intelligent and sincere about his work. Whom do you think the Boss will continue to pressurize about the work more? If it's time to assign another work load, whom will the Boss assign it? Why? Consider the pain of motivating the incompetent person versus the ease of using the existing hard working employee.*
2. *A student has received an assignment which is due for submission on the midnight of the seventh day from now. There is a penalty for late submission. When is the right*

time to do the assignment? When does it get done usually? Why? Consider the pain of doing the homework versus the ease of postponing it.

3. One who would hardly want to spend $2 on a bottle of water might happily pay double the price at an airport, in a cinema hall or at a stadium. Why? Consider the inconvenience or pain in the moment versus pain of an extra sum of money spent.

4. People sign up for free trial. Why? Once the trial period ends many continue the membership ending up paying for something which was never intended in the beginning. Why? Consider the advantage at the time of signing up and pain later at the time of cancelling due to certain habit and attachment with product and services offered.

5. You see the campaign about global warming which will eventually make polar ice to melt and submerge the continents in ocean. Or you see the message about rivers drying up and that only 50% of drinking water need will be available by 2030. What do you do? You see a message about the last day of the 50% deal at Macy's. What do you do? Why? Which death is more powerful – lost opportunity in present moment or the probability of death in distant future?

6. An employee works very hard and asks for raise to his Boss on various occasions citing his achievements and contribution to the group. The Boss doesn't pay much attention. Why? Consider the pain of losing some of the budget money with no additional benefit in present moment.

   a. The employee finally gets another job offer and resigns. The Boss offers him a big raise to stay with the company. Why? Consider the pain of losing a working employee versus losing some of the budget money in retaining the employee.

Mind, the Player

Mind is a playful, pattern seeking and easy going mechanism

Neera was surprised in the same way as I had been for many years. One would think that humans, who have been educated, professionally trained and have been operating highly critical operations in various fields of life would be making decisions based on the facts, data and rationality. Contrary to the expectation, they end up making all the decisions based on their personal evaluation of fears and pains. It seemed that everything the humans did in this world was plainly driven by the *mind*. Mind, the universal mechanism, exists everywhere and seems to drive all the movements. Or, it won't be wrong to say that the *mind is the movement* that exists universally and all forms of living creation are nothing but its manifestation. Trying to avoid pain in the present moment is just one of the characteristic of the mind. It is not difficult to see that all kinds of human beings with different level of education, training and experience behave in almost the same way. Everyone wants to be safe, is afraid to lose and desires to possess more, a behavior pattern seen in all creatures. It is as if the mind, which is the universal movement, is the main driving mechanism for humans too, having taken a lead over the high intellect capability of their brain.

Neera wanted to know more. She didn't want to continue living the way most humans seemed, unaware and mechanical. If humans could not utilize the high intellect capability of their brain to take care of the most crucial decisions in life, it was a waste. It would be lame to buy a super computer and use it to do simple addition and multiplications which even a cheap calculator could do. If the decision making capability of a smart human was not different than a parrot, sparrow or a fish, then there was something terribly wrong. No matter how intelligent solution to any situation existed that benefitted the whole world, an alternative solution gets picked for a petty little advantage to a petty little human in some far corner of the earth. What could be the reason? Is it that the mind is something more powerful than human intellect? If that was the case, why would a few highly intelligent people exist in the world? Or is it that the mind is the most difficult thing to understand, or taking charge of? The answers would not be possible unless we tried to find out everything about the mind. I was sure that when we came to know everything about the mind, it would be easier to stop letting it control the way we lead our lives, totally unaware, totally selfish, totally separate.

Neera was ready to go to the next level. The observation, movement and the corresponding actions seemed to be nothing but the working of the mind. The task of understanding the mind was as tricky as it is for a policeman to catch the thief when the thief was none other than the policeman itself. When the mind controls every little movement of the universe, it becomes tricky to identify if the new gained knowledge is a work of the mind or really some new insight. Nevertheless, we decided to explore the world of mind from what was observable and available for analysis and keep our doubts aside for the time being.

I told to Neera, "We talked about observation, movement, and appropriate action so far. And we also discussed that the action was dependent on the perception of pain or death in the moment. We called this mechanism of the movement as the mind, which seems to be the sum total of everything observed, sensed or noticed in the universe. It makes sense to imagine this one thing as the origin or base of all movements, because then it becomes clear that only one kind of rule should have existed governing all movements."

Neera said, "So we wish to talk about its nature, qualities and its characteristics; its predictability in different kinds of situations."

I said, "Yes. Contrary to one's expectation, the study of the mind and its characteristics is the simplest thing. When you know that it is something that drives every living being, all you have to do is to observe."

Neera asked, "Just observe? What exactly do we observe? Whom do we observe?"

I said, "Not what or whom. Just observe. Observe everything; not any one or a few things in particular."

Neera asked, "And what do we find when we observe?"

I said, "We observe that the universe contains all kinds of creatures. There are some organisms with as little as one single cell. There are other kinds of creatures which have hardly one or two kinds of senses. On the extreme end there are human beings with multiple sensory organs and a brain to think, store and process information. We observe that the whole universe seems to operate on the single principle, that is to move in order to avoid pain or death."

Neera asked, "Isn't the universe operating perfectly fine? Why do we need to investigate what's the rule guiding this universe? What exactly do we want to change or improve?"

I replied, "Didn't we observe in our last discussion that a human mind if far more capable of understanding a situation than a primitive counterpart in this universe. Yet, when it comes to decision making, humans seem to make the decisions based on their survival instincts. The masses continue to choose a leader who failed them many times in the past, a manager in a company continues to promote incompetent employees and an average person continues to eat unhealthy food even when made aware of the imminent harms. The most intelligent species on this earth continue to operate in survival mode, making decisions in order to avoid pain, suffering and inconvenience as if it is like a death."

Neera asked, "So you mean to say we want to know what all mysterious ways does the mind works just like this particular behavior that seems so unfitting to the intelligent species?"

I said, "Yes, because *observation is action* (Rule:10). When you observe, notice or know about something completely, then the appropriate action happens."

Neera spoke with a little bit of surprise, "Papa, isn't it unusual? We said that observation is followed by an appropriate action. But isn't it the nature of the mind to act immediately based on its perception of reward or punishments?"

I said, "Yes, that is the nature of the mind."

Neera said, "So we want to study about the mind so completely, that when we have observed it fully, the appropriate action happens automatically. You mean to say we use the mind to study the mind and then leave it to fix itself automatically!"

She then asked, "So what all do we observe in the mind? So far we have found out that it is scared of death."

I said, "There are a lot of things about the mind besides this but let's first discuss more about this very basic quality of the mind. We said that the mind is driven towards the pleasures and away from pain and destruction. We already talked about the meaning of pain and pleasures. We said that they are not two different feelings but the single quality seen as two by the *relativity between the two*. In other words, *a lesser pain is same as more pleasure.*"

I continued, "When we say that the mind moves such that it *avoids the pain and destruction* (Rule:11,13), this can also mean that the mind *wants to continue forever*. What does it mean when something wants to continue forever? When something *fears* death, it feels *insecure* and tries to take a *safe* decision. A mind feels safe and secure with the things that it already knows about. It feels insecure with unknown. A fearful mind *afraid of unknown* continues to stick with the *known*, which means that a mind burdened with knowledge and conditioning continues to become more and more lethargic and *lazy*. When faced with two choices, one of them being difficult, the conditioned mind feels safe with the *simple* one. Feeling lazy the mind continues to *simplify* complex situations for an easier tomorrow. This lazy nature manifests into the *habit* making nature of the mind, which after a few attempts tends to create habits. Once made into a habit, the act becomes known, safe and an integrated part of the mind. A habit is the way of the mind to integrate with universal infinite energy. Every human being can be seen doing what he or she is habitual of doing; tirelessly! Afraid of unknown, the mind has a tendency to hold on to the fixed and stable ground, an *anchor*. It is like moving a mountain to ask someone to leave the comforts of their language, culture, country or religion; they are the anchors that the mind attaches to. Being afraid of death and destruction, the mind wants to continue *growing* and *expanding*. The urge to grow and expand in order to protect and retain itself manifests as *greed* and *restlessness*. Mind achieves its growth by making its *copies* and *replicating* itself by way of *extension* and *inheritance*. The process of making copies or replicating requires mind an ability of *memorizing, recognizing,* and *comparing* patterns. It has an ability of recognizing patterns and forms by *identifying* through *symbols* and *names*. The fear and *insecurity* is reflected in the need of the mind *to be in control* all the time. It doesn't like to be controlled or bound, unless the bondage becomes a habit. In short, this is all a mind is."

Neera was listening. She didn't know what to say. The nature of the mind was basically all of the personality of a human being. The same mind is fresh, energetic, and artistic in a child and yet, completely lethargic, conditioned and burdened with memories in an adult. The same mind which manifests itself in all kinds of movements is seen so different and contrasting in every new movement. The same mind which had been there billions of years ago and will continue to remain for an indefinite time, is both fresh and stale at the same time. It is fresh because it is changing and evolving in present moment based on its analysis of threats and rewards. It is stale because it is making decisions based on its previous experiences and habits. The insecurity of the mind paradoxically wants it to grow as well as wants it to hold on the fixed anchor. It wants to grow because it is insecure and fearful of facing destruction. It holds on to a fixed anchor because it is insecure of the unknown outside the realm of the known anchor. It simplifies as well as complicates things. It simplifies the situations containing more information than it can process. It complicates when things are so simple that they don't offer any challenge. A mind seemed nothing but a paradox. It was all puzzling, mesmerizing, baffling. Neera's mind was echoing all the characteristics of the mind, reflecting and pondering on its nature.

Picture: 9.1 Nature of the Mind

I asked Neera, "So where would you start talking about the mind?"

Neera said, "I would like to start about its lazy nature and its tendency to go for making things simpler."

I said, "The first thing to understand is that the lazy nature doesn't mean lethargic or non-moving. By calling it lazy, we mean to say that it is not serious; it is *easy going, playful* by nature. The mind does not want things to be tiring, full of effort, forceful or labor oriented. For mind, everything should be like a play, a fun activity. Look at a dog, a cat or any other creature. If not eating or relaxing, they are just playing. A play never tires them, in the sense that it never brings boredom. The same playful mind is the core driver of all humans too, which can be seen in all children. Most adults have got this playful mind suppressed because of heavy conditioning and habitual nature forced by education, religion and enforcement of social culture. It is easy to see any child and a parent, the child is always playful while the adult is always stopping it from being playful, slowly conditioning it to become lethargic, conditioned and forgetful of its natural tendencies. Let us list down how this lazy or playful nature is manifested as some of its unique traits."

Neera grabbed the notebook and started to write as I listed the key characteristics emerging from being easy going and playful.

> ### The easy going mind
> - Understands patterns; assigns symbols and names to patterns and forms
> - Stores the symbols & names in memory; retrieves in future for ease
> - Handles only a few objects at a time; when faces many objects, it integrates them together

I started talking how the easy going nature of the mind reflects in the extremely smart ways various actions get performed. Neera was observant and silently listening. I told her how the mind is wired to understand patterns. A pattern is a collection of different objects arranged in repetitive or symmetric manner. When faced with multiple objects in an observation, the mind doesn't view them individually, but integrates the whole view. The process of integration or merging of visible distinctions or contrast gives rise to what seems as shapes and patterns. Mind understands patterns very well and has ability to remember and recall the previously observed patterns immediately. A pattern can be observed when a single object moves through time. It can also be observed when multiple objects are arranged spatially or move through space and time. A mind is at ease with any kind of pattern, whether simple or highly complex. In short, it can be said that *Mind is pattern* itself.

Neera asked me to give her some examples of patterns that can be simple as well as complex in terms of time and space. I thought of taking the simplest one, a circle.

A circle, according to the dictionary is "a closed plane curve consisting of all points at a given distance from a point within it called the center." It is rather confusing for someone to understand the meaning of this definition and get an absolutely clear idea about a circle. If I were to explain a circle to someone for the first time, I would say a circle is this.

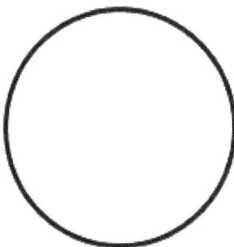

Picture: 9.2 All patterns similar to this are known as circles

The mind has the ability to observe the above picture and *recognize* it at other time or other location. Given two such shapes, the mind can *compare* the two and understand the differences between the two. It also possesses another unique quality of *association* of two different such recognitions. Once it trains itself to identify such shape with a symbol called 'circle', it need not observe the shape anymore to recall, recognize or compare. All it needs is a reference through the symbol and it *recreates* the pattern.

The above shape is the ideal form observed, associated with a name and remembered by the mind. Any pattern in space, time or space time giving a resemblance with this shape is perceived by the mind as a circle, known as a circle and is treated as a circle. For example, a few colored pencils are arranged in the picture 9.3 such that the mind integrates all the tips and perceives the arrangement as a circle. Once it perceives the pattern as a circle, it calls it a circle and treats it as a circle as well.

Picture: 9.3 The Mind sees a circle in spatial arrangement

In another scenario, an object may not itself be in a shape of circle, but moves in a path which is similar to a circle. When the movement is fast, the mind integrates the visible motion and merges it into a single picture, which looks like a circle. For example, the following is a ceiling fan, which is nowhere close to the shape of a circle, when moves, creates an impression of a circle. This is one way in which a movement in time gives rise to a pattern.

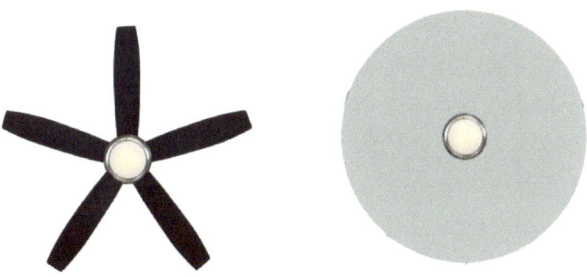

Picture: 9.4 The Mind sees a circle through movement in time

The mind has the ability to perceive and recognize patterns in both space and time. It can understand shapes as well as sequences. It can understand simple linear sequences as well as complex sequence of curves. The mind not only understands the curvy motion signifying a sequence in time, but can predict the probable trajectory of a moving object too. In the following example, understanding the current pattern sequence, recognizing the trend and predicting an extension to this trend is an ability that all the minds understand.

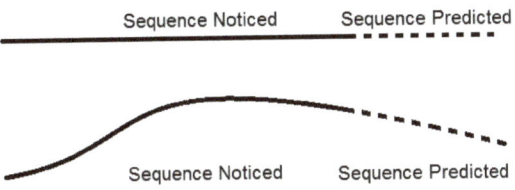

Picture: 9.5 Mind has an ability to predict sequence

The ability to understand and predict such complex sequence involving movement through time is not just a human privilege. It is easily known and understood by mind in all forms of existence throughout the universe. Throw a piece of a bread in air and a crow can catch it in mid-air showing the understanding of the complex time based parabolic trajectory made by the flying food. A dog does not need special training to catch a flying saucer or a ball in mid-air. A chasing cheetah trying to catch a deer taking rapid turns makes appropriate adjustments to its own trajectory without a formal training. The mind knows the patterns and sequences; mind itself is a pattern. There is no concept of any simple or complicated pattern for a mind. If a pattern is observed, the mind can operate on it by remembering, naming, recalling and comparing with ease.

Picture: 9.6 The Mind has an understanding of complex time based parabolic trajectory and predicting future path

Neera asked, "And if I am guessing right, this doesn't involve only seeing but all other senses too!"

I said, "You have guessed right! What we call as music is a pattern. If not a pattern, the sound is simply noise to the ears. Being a pattern, music tends to be identified with symbols or keywords, remembered and replayed at will. The music, as we all know, is understood by many other species too. As long as any observable movement follows some pattern or a sequence, the mind is able to grasp it. Once a pattern is grasped, the mind can learn, memorize and recreate at its will."

The mind does not differentiate between a shape or a pattern from its reflection or mirror image. To a mind, the shape is still the same. When a child is being taught how to write, it doesn't see an 'R' different from 'Я'. When a child plays a game of arranging the alphabet shapes into their corresponding slots, it finds no difficulty in picking up the alphabets with face down. The inverted shape of the character is seen and recognized without any effort. A child's mind is the pure mind; a mind without conditioning. We make a lot of effort in conditioning a pure mind, so that it can fit into a standard pattern of the population.

Picture: 9.7 An unconditioned mind is not confused by mirror images

A mind understands sound and other sensory patterns as easy as visual ones. When faced with a particular piece of music heard initially in the sound of a violin, the mind can recognize the same pattern even if played with a different instrument such as a piano or a trumpet. A mind can associate songs with their tunes and can recognize even if hummed by someone. Mind understands the visual patterns in the same way. Once familiar with alphabets of a language, the mind can understand the letters written in thousands of different handwritings. It is the pattern that the mind cares for, all other variations surrounding the central pattern are simply ignored.

Mind, being one with the patterns and sequences is at ease with music, stories, and numbers in many interesting ways. It can sort random arrangements of objects and put them in orderly manner. Fluent in understanding, remembering and recalling the patterns, copying and imitating are its inherent qualities. The mind can copy or imitate itself because it can remember the patterns. With an ability to copy or imitate, mind is able to grow and expand at its will.

Give an incomplete pattern to the mind, and it will try to complete it once it understands the pattern. Children play with interest with such toys as blocks and shapes where they are able to understand a sequence and complete it in the right way. This tendency of completing the unfinished patterns manifests as the mind's tendency to repair broken things.

Mind doesn't need a completely ideal pattern or sequence in order to recognize or repeat a pattern or a sequence. A slight variation in a pattern is ignored and the overall pattern is still seen as a similar pattern. A written word with a spelling mistake is recognized as easily as the one without a mistake. Every human face is different, yet all are recognized as human faces. There are hundreds of different models of telephone in the market, but the mind recognizes them all as phones by looking at the key pattern being the same in all of them. A pattern can be slowly changed over time in such a way that the mind never recognizes the change. In due course, the original pattern can be completely changed into a new form, and the mind will not be able to realize when the original pattern got to become completely different. When one sees one's sons, daughters grow slowly over the years; one doesn't stop recognizing them as one's own children. But anyone who has seen the same children a few years ago will fail to recognize them because they would have completely changed. This characteristic of the mind is used to control the minds of the masses by introducing them to any big changes so slowly that they fail to realize themselves being controlled.

I thought it was the time to make things a bit serious for Neera. I asked her, "Now that you know that the mind inherently understands patterns and finds working with them as one of its innate qualities, how do you think humans have exploited it to their own *misfortune*?"

Neera asked, "Do you mean to say that humans have known that the mind can be exploited by feeding it patterned behavior?"

I said, "Yes. Once it is seen that all humans have a tendency to understand patterns and can be made to mold to machine-like behavior, it seems to be the obvious choice. All minds are the same; what works for one can work for all. One scientist named Ivan Pavlov had experimented with his dog where he rang a bell every time he served food to the dog. When the process was repeatedly observed, the dog (the mind) learned the pattern (ringing of bell followed by the food). The mind (of the dog) was so conditioned that the dog started salivating on the sound of the bell itself, even when it was not served food. Humans too are conditioned in the same way as they can unconsciously be made to follow some pattern to make them habituated."

Neera said, "Papa, I remember something funny that I read on the social media. It mentioned that once Pavlov was sitting in a bar when the bartender rang the bell. Pavlov suddenly stood up saying it must be the time to feed the dog!"

I laughed. It was funny, yet an eye opener. The mind can easily see the patterns everywhere, but it fails to see its own patterned behavior. The *Observer can't observe itself* (Rule:5). It was true that if the ringing of bell and offering of food was a pattern for the dog, it was a pattern for Pavlov too. We easily observe and follow patterns and sequences everywhere, but fail to see our own patterned and conditioned behavior. My thoughts were interrupted by Neera's question, "Papa, you were saying something about exploitation of humans by making them conditioned."

I said, "I have used the word exploitation here, though, all the people will not think they are being exploited. When one hears a national anthem, one rises up with a feeling of pride in one's heart. When one hears the bell from a temple or church, one immediately senses rising of an emotion or feeling. A student hears the morning roll-call bell and immediately moves to the playground to avoid getting punished. It is all simply mind, behaving what it has been *trained* to do by repeated enforcement and conditioning."

Neera asked, "So what is the reason we get conditioned to behave mechanically?"

I said, "Let's write down the process of conditioning of mind". I wrote.

Conditioning of the Mind
- *Observation* of movement, pattern or sequence
- *Association* of the pattern or sequence with a symbol
- *Recollecting* the pattern or sequence on observing the symbol

Neera asked, "Isn't making good habits desirable? Why do you say that all conditioning is exploitation?"

I said, "What is good for one may not be good for other. Who decides something good for the masses? A conditioned response is never intelligent. It is always the same irrespective of the situation. How can some intelligent entity behave the same way in all conditions and still not see the stupidity of such action? If you are conditioned to hate some kind of food, you will remain hateful for the food in all situations. Once you associate the hate to the food, you will hate those people too who eat that food. In the same way if you have been conditioned to feel a language as inferior to your own, you will feel all people as inferior who are using that language. You will find all the literature inferior which is written in that language. Do you see why I say that the capacity of the mind to be easily molded into patterns is the biggest way any living being can be exploited?"

Neera said, "I can see what you are suggesting. You are trying to say that when we are conditioned to behave in a particular way, we are not observant, not aware. Any act done unaware cannot be an intelligent act. *A conditioned mind is not intelligent mind."*

I said, "A knife is a wonderful tool to have, but has its own risks when used carelessly. Likewise the mind has a great capability only as long as it is not allowed to wander aimlessly. The power and ease of mind to use symbols is immense. Like a magic spell, with one word, sound or a symbol the mind can recreate the whole associated pattern or sequence along with emotions. To a mind, a symbol is same as the pattern it is associated with."

Neera interrupted me, "Wait! I want to understand what you just said. A symbol is same as the idea, thought, memory or pattern it represents?"

I said, "Yes, this is one of the biggest mysteries of the mind. *To a mind, a symbol is no different than the pattern it is associated with.* A sound of bell makes the Pavlov dog salivate. For him the sound of bell represents the food, so the sound of bell *is the food."*

Neera said, "Oh, You did mention it just now, but I failed to appreciate the important thought behind this. I want to know more. This is so wonderful!"

I said, "Mind is symbols. If X represents a thing, then X is same as the thing. One may not be bothered if a piece of paper is burned in front of him. If the same paper happens to symbolize the currency he understands, he will find it strange and feel sad for the waste. If the same paper happens to symbolize the flag of the country he associates himself with, he may become emotional, aggressive or even murderous. A symbol is not different than the thing it represents. A symbol of a flag is a symbol of the country one associates with; a country is another symbol one associates with as a matter of pride, honor and worth killing or dying for."

I continued, "A word is a symbol too. It is associated with its interpretations. Using a word is same as using all that the word conveys. This is how language works. In reality a word is just a symbol. *A word is not the thing.* But we have accustomed of using symbols to such a large extent that we get energized and aggressive on hearing some words that we don't like. A word is all that it conveys; if the word is a representative of an abuse, the word is an abuse. The mind does not discriminate between the word and the idea it's associated with. *A word is the thing for the unaware mind.*"

I didn't see Neera interrupting and I didn't care if she didn't. It was not a matter of debate or even a discussion that she would think of asking any questions. It was so simple, straightforward and a known weakness of all of us, which we were never made aware of by any book or a person before. I said, "The very first encounter to any movement is a fresh encounter because there is no previous knowledge or memory to cloud the observation. But as soon as the movement and the associated pattern or action, experience and emotions are observed, it is stored in the memory as knowledge. A later encounter with the same symbol allows the mind to recreate the memory and relate it to the known experience. Let us imagine a child having a chance to see and play with a balloon for the first time. It finds the soft round colorful balloon fun to play with. A few more encounters with the balloons on some birthday parties, and the child learns to associate the balloons to the birthday parties. When such a child sees the balloon in future, it does not play with it with as much interest as it played with it on its first encounter. A balloon is now a symbol for the funs of a birthday parties for the child. Instead, it looks around to find where the party is."

Neera said, "Yes, this is true. Balloons tend to become a decoration, a symbol for the party rather than a thing to play with."

I said, "It's not just with the child. A few more such encounters, and the mind gets more mature and solidified with its symbol. If such a mind encounters balloons (Being colorful, prominent and animated, they continue to grab attention) and it sees that there are no parties around, it doesn't ignore them. It still knows that a balloon is a symbol for something; if there is no party, there must be something worth paying an attention. The advertisers know this, and they have been successfully able to draw the attention of a casual unaware mind to their presence."

Neera asked, "Is there any limit on how big a symbol should be for an idea of pattern depending on its simplicity or complexity? Can a dot on a paper symbolize a thing as complex as a galaxy?"

I asked, "Is it not true? Don't the dots on the sky mean the whole galaxies to you? Once you are told by the science books that each dot you see might be millions of miles away and might be millions of times bigger than our planet earth, doesn't the mind accept the truth and starts taking those dots in the sky as huge planets, stars and galaxies?"

Neera said, "How stupid of me. In fact, I realized this the moment I stated my question to you. A symbol can represent anything from infinity to eternity. The mind doesn't mind."

I said, "It happened just last week. There was a tiny dot moving on the skies of Arizona in the evening. I along with most of the residents of Arizona wouldn't bother to care even if we noticed the moving dot in the sky. There were far brighter dots moving in the sky as it was the time for the aircrafts to make their landing on the nearby airport. One of our friends was extremely excited about this moving dot, which was not even bright or much interesting to look at. He was excited, because he was closely following the path of the International Space Station (ISS), and this dot was nothing but that. To him the dot was the ISS; for everybody else unaware of such knowledge it was just an insignificant dot. For the mind, a symbol is the same as the thing associated."

I continued, "A symbol or a token may be any physical or a mental object. A piece of paper, plastic or wood may be exchanged with any object on the planet. You are aware this is how a currency or a legal deed works. You may possess a few piles of papers, and you are considered the wealthiest and the most powerful person on the earth. A promise is a mental or an imaginary symbol that could be exchanged with anything else in this world. A mind does not care what the exact nature of a symbol is. If a symbol is assigned to a pattern, the symbol is the pattern."

It was Neera's time to open up. She said, "I know something on the similar lines. I love talking to my elder sister. I know how she looks and sounds as I have been living with her forever. The mind has associated her looks, her sound and her presence with her name. The mind even knows the close association of the written name with the sound of the spoken name, and it can associate it with my sister. When I hear a sound on the phone, I immediately know I am talking to my sister. The sound of my sister is my sister. The looks of my sister is my sister. The mind immediately replaces the sound that I hear on my phone to the idea of my sister. Taking it further, when I read a letter sent by her, I can recognize her handwriting and know that she has written the message to me. When I read the message, I know that she is talking to me. The mind associates the special pattern of written message to my sister. The handwritten message of my sister is my sister. These days even when she types the letters on a printer, the mind can relate the machine printed words in standard font to my sister, because of the envelope that mentions her name as the sender. A signature at the bottom of a message is symbolic of the whole message belonging to the person symbolized by the signature. The mind is strange; it can relate to a symbol representing another symbol representing another symbol and can continue like this forever with getting confused, tired and lost. These days a chat message or an email from an identity works just the same way, a text on the phone is same as if it is spoken by the person in person."

"The mind is nothing but the symbols and their interpretations. As we said, a token may represent a currency of a nation. The currency may symbolize its worth equal to another physical object. Any person will be happy to exchange one symbol for the other object, because the mind knows that a symbol is the same thing as the idea it represents. A piece of paper with standard contractual wordings may be equivalent to a villa on a beach front. The symbolic value of a villa on a beach front may be equivalent to the status of a person being wealthy. The wealthy status of a person may represent the person as being powerful. A single piece of paper may symbolize anything and everything on this planet and beyond. The mind is nothing but just symbol and its association with some patterns, sequences or ideas." I continued reiterating the significance of symbols for the mind.

Neera said, "I am getting a feel of what you have said. It is so funny and ridiculous. I have a friend in my class. His name is Shiva. He is in love with Rajnikant, the super hero of

South-Indian movies. Since he loves Rajnikant, he also loves a tweet from Rajnikant; a tweet of Rajnikant is (like) Rajnikant itself. He loves a shirt that Rajnikant wore in one of his movies; a shirt of Rajnikant is (like) Rajnikant itself. Given an opportunity, he might even buy that same shirt from some auction for thousands of dollars. He loves red color because Rajnikant loves red color too; the choices of Rajnikant is (like) Rajnikant itself. A symbol is like the thing. A symbol is same as the thing. *A symbol is the thing.*"

I could see the Neera slowly understood that for a mind, dealing with some symbolic representation was not just an idea; it was a reality. I asked, "Don't you see it as a beginning of wisdom? Do you realize the inherent quality of the mind to take any idea to infinity and beyond? Do you see how weak a human is, to be in the hands of the mind which knows no bounds? It just doesn't know where to stop." The fact is that the mind not only symbolizes some identified patterns or sequences for simplicity, it even treats the symbols as if they are the things they represent. It is a well-known example in the ancient Hindu scriptures where this quality of the mind is reflected in an example of rope and a snake. It is mentioned that if the mind takes some rope as a snake, it actually gets fearful. The idea of a snake is not different than a real snake; they both result in an immediate action, the one born out of the threat to the life by recognizing a dangerous situation. Once the mind clearly observes the thing seen as a rope, the fear is vanished. A rule began to emerge.

Rule 16: There is no difference between a thing and an idea of the thing for the mind.

"Do you want to hear more examples of how the mind searching for short-cuts and ease of decision making hijacks the intellectual capability of humans?" I asked Neera.

Neera said, "Yes, even though I have understood how the symbols are seen same as the pattern they represent in terms of reality, I won't get tired of hearing more about it."

I said, "Look at another such example. In the car markets, many manufacturers established themselves as luxury car makers by offering sophisticated features in their cars such as better suspension, leather seats, automatic climate controls, precise edges and high quality manufacturing. Soon people learned to associate their name and company logo to the sophistication they provided. When someone drove a car that displayed a logo of Mercedes, Audi or BMW, he was seen as a person of wealth and influence. The mind learns to adapt fast, and within no time, all it knew was that these names and logos were representative of luxury, class and prestige. The world progressed fast and technology improved over the years, and every car maker started providing about the same level of luxury by providing radios, music systems, leather, automatic drives, air-conditioning and comfortable ride. The mind has a habit of habit-making and it cannot let go the symbols it created over a period of time. Many people still take some company names and logos as a representation of luxury and so those who cannot afford to buy expensive models end up buying cheaper models of those companies recognized for their luxury status. The irony is that such people end up buying the cheaper and less luxurious models of those brands that the mind thinks as the symbol of luxury even though other companies which do not symbolize of luxury or class offer more luxury for lesser price. The lazy mind cannot let go the symbol of luxury and takes the symbol as luxury itself. A person today feels pride in driving a cheaper model of Mercedes or Audi compared to someone who drives an expensive and luxurious model of Honda, even though they might be similarly priced."

Neera said, "I know. I find it funny when I take a symbol of luxury as luxury, and not so much to the luxury itself. It seems, the mind takes its infatuation with symbols to such heights that *symbols mean more than the things they stand for*."

I was surprised with what Neera just said. It never occurred to me before. All this time I was trying to say that a symbol was the thing itself, and here she said that a symbol was more real than the reality. It was a great revelation. As I thought more and more, it became evident as the truth. For centuries, people of various faiths have symbolized their beliefs in God through different symbols. Hindus believe in various forms of gods and worship them in form of statues and pictures in temples and homes. The belief in the symbolic form of God is to such a great extent that the symbol means more to them than the real thing it stands for. They would die in order to protect the symbols, even though a symbol by itself should not mean anything. A symbol is like an image in the mirror; you may try to hit the image but it cannot do any harm to the real object. Those attached to the symbols don't see the facts in the light of rational arguments; to them a symbol is more of a God than the God itself. Neera was right. It was more of a rule, it seemed.

Rule 17: Symbols mean more than the things or ideas they symbolize.

Neera said, "Papa, isn't everything in this world driven just by symbolic ideas? I don't think anyone cares to look at the things as they exist. In the limited time available, everybody holds on to preconceived ideas, prejudices and symbolic representations in order to evaluate the reality. At an interview, the clothes and looks will symbolize many obvious interpretations and someone without proper attire will not be taken seriously. Their clothes will symbolize who they are, more than they themselves. A well written resume will have more impact than ordinarily written resume. The format, language, arrangement and the keywords will decide if the candidate is going to be shortlisted for the interview, even if everything in the description is a lie. There are thousands of experts advising everyone to write better resumes, because a well written resume is a better candidate than the candidate itself. This laziness of the mind is very well understood by shrewd people, thieves, imposters, politicians, magicians, businessmen and artists. They influence the masses by taking advantage of this weakness by means of manipulating their clothes, language, accent, behavior and personality."

I said, "In short, the mind holds on to symbols and names in place of the things and ideas those symbols and names stand for. To a mind, a symbol is more real than the reality. What we call as learning, knowledge and education is simply our conditioning by the social institutions by making us learn different symbols and their associations in the fields of science, religion and social interchange. In order to be free of conditioning, the mind will have to become aware of this shortcoming. A pure observation devoid of any conditioning is the key to end this deep sleep of unawareness."

> **The mind holds on to symbols and names in place of the things and ideas those symbols and names stand for. To a mind, a symbol is more real than the reality.**

Neera asked, "So the mind makes things easier by means of recognizing and remembering patterns, assigning symbols and using symbols in place of the original patterns. You also mentioned about mind's inability to handle more than a few things at a time. How does it handle the immense information available to it every moment?"

I said smilingly, "We will take it up next time; too much to handle."

Neera understood the joke. She smiled.

10

Memory, Known & the Backdrop

Memory of the known creates the backdrop,
the conditioning which corrupts the
observation

We were saying that the mind has unlimited information at every moment, and given that it thrives for easier alternatives, it needs some way out. The mind is brilliantly smart; it knows what changed and what has not. What has not changed doesn't need its attention. The attention is always on what is changing. The non-changing is the backdrop. As the time progresses, the noticing of the current changes or the movement becomes the part of the known. Once known, a change doesn't need mind's attention as it becomes part of the stored knowledge, memory and therefore the backdrop. The backdrop of memory or acquired knowledge continuously gets built up so that the mind is always looking at the incremental change, from what has already been known.

I and Neera in the past few weeks had developed this thought by carefully discussing about the movements, observations and observer. We had also found out that the observation could either be unconditioned and fresh or conditioned with the past memory and therefore old. I didn't want to repeat all the reasoning about how the observer was the background itself, as we had already understood that part. An unconditional observation was a blank backdrop with no memory of the past. On the other side, a conditioned observation was always burdened with the memory of the past. We had noted further that if an observation was tied up with an appropriate action, the happening of the action was automatic, immediate, and full of energy. It was the quality of the observation that determined the quality of the following action; a conditioned observation would result in a conditioned action. For example, a mind burdened with the deep rooted knowledge of nationality would react in a strong manner when it notices a symbolic flag being damaged by someone intentionally or unintentionally.

I asked Neera, "Do you remember we drew some flowchart on observation and corresponding action some time back?"

Neera said, "Yes. And I do remember that we had made those figures without considering the element of past memory and experiences of the observer."

I said, "Right. I hope you already understood that the memory does play important part in refreshing the backdrop, the observer, so that the mind doesn't have to process all the information it has already known in the past."

Neera said, "I know. When you introduced the long and boring example of the plain sheet of paper and the little mouse on the corner of the page, we had seen how soon the newly acquired knowledge became the part of the known, and therefore stale, unnecessary and boring."

I said, "The universal mind seems to be operating without support of the memory, but the humans, who have such an advanced mind, have heavily depended on the past knowledge for further observation and exploration. It would be worthwhile to understand how we humans observe and therefore act differently in this universe. So, do you want to update our picture about an observation which happens in presence of the memory?"

Neera said, "Yes, I can understand how useful it would be. I think, I do understand how to make those diagrams." She modified the picture of the comparator model of observation of a movement by adding a storage element depicting memory. She connected the output back to input through an element of memory which stored accumulated memory as well as presented a knowledge-based frame of reference working as a backdrop.

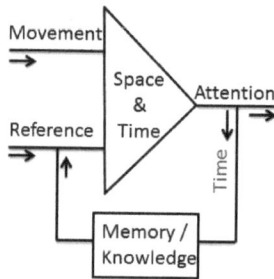

Picture: 10.1 Conditioned Observation of a Movement

The picture was simple and complete. As an attention falls on a movement, it becomes part of memory and knowledge, a process that takes time. As the observation continues the reference gets modified with the updated backdrop of knowledge and memory. As new information continues to become old in the process of memory and knowledge building, the mind continues to be restless, trying to 'look' for another movement. A mind which continues to thrive for new excitement, new task to avoid the boredom is a conditioned mind. *A mind with no memory of the old can never get bored*, because all the movement under observation is always fresh. Humans have long lost the 'art' of dropping the memory in order to become content and at peace, the art of doing nothing.

I asked Neera to modify the observation-action duo also for a mind conditioned with memory of the past. She modified the previous drawing with memory element added to it.

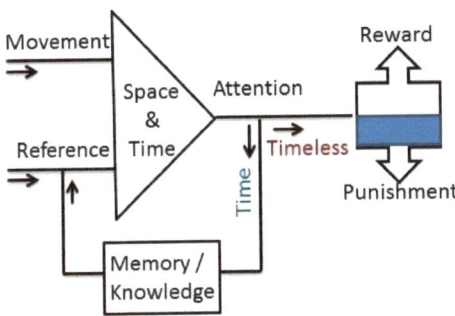

Picture: 10.2 Conditioned Observation-Action Pair

The picture showed all the elements of observation-action pair. The left section represented observation and building up of a conditioning, something that takes place in time. The right section showed timeless action as a response to the nature of observation, irrespective of whether it was a conditioned or unconditioned one. I asked Neera if she could explain the examples we discussed so far about observation of movements with reference to this picture.

She said, "I think we talked about different cases of observation-action pair. This is how I could recapitulate a couple of them.

As a child who has no memory or knowledge about a scorpion, when it notices a movement, it may try to go near and catch hold of it. In *due course of time* when it acquires knowledge about a scorpion being deadly through books or other people it becomes part of memory and knowledge. In due course of time, when the same person observes a scorpion, it *immediately* acts as a natural response to the observation, either killing it or running away from it.

As a child or as someone with a different nationality, when someone notices a symbol of flag on a paper being torn or burned, it does not get affected seriously. Later, in due course of time, when the same person acquires knowledge about the nationality and symbol of pride, it acts immediately in response to the destruction of the symbol.

I think, it is pretty much clear that the appropriate action following an observation is always timeless, irrespective of whether the observation is conditioned or unconditioned. A response resulting out of watching a snake, or one's national flag burned, or touching a hot surface or being insulted is always immediate; a timeless action." Thus she summarized her observations on the behavior of the mind.

I told Neera, "It seems that now we understand how a backdrop works as the frame of reference for further observations. We said that the mind works this way to make things simple for itself; otherwise it won't be possible to capture the infinite movements happening all the time. There is another way the mind makes things easier for itself. It is by way of integrating all the observed movements as one".

Neera said, "I remember I asked you what happens when there are many colorful objects in the field of observation.

You gave an example of many red colored windows and showed that all of them were noticed at the same time."

I said, "Exactly! When there are similar multiple movements, all are seen as one, in an integrated manner. In the example of windows you mentioned, the object of attention was the set of all red windows. The mind does not care to count or consider all the individual objects observed in a given moment. Instead, it builds up an integrated sum of all observed movements at once. This integrated mass may become the backdrop if the attention continues to remain and there are further movements noticed."

"I don't understand the last part." Neera asked, "What do you mean when you say that the integrated mass becomes the new backdrop?"

I said, "If you remember, when you remained with the blank paper with a little mouse in the corner for some time, the paper with the mouse became a new backdrop. In a short time, you were looking for further movement because the knowledge about last movement was already acquired."

Neera said, "That's right. The backdrop continues to get updated with the new knowledge".

I said, "In case of multiple objects becoming the field of attention, there are chances that another movement may happen while the attention is still on the integrated sum of objects. This new movement happens to be seen from the backdrop of integrated sum of recently noticed movement."

Neera said, "I think I might understand it, but you would need to explain this to me with a couple of examples."

I said, "When you look at the picture, you immediately notice all the red windows on the building on one floor."

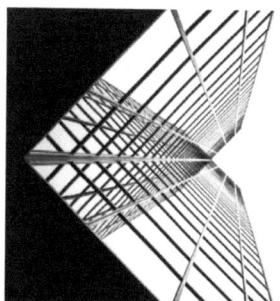 

Picture: 10.3 Similarities tend to be make a close group

Neera said, "That is right. We notice all of the red windows together, as an integrated entity, *a set of all red windows.*"

I asked Neera, "Before your attention has had a chance to move away, if one of the windows opened so that its red color is not noticeable, what you say you noticed?"

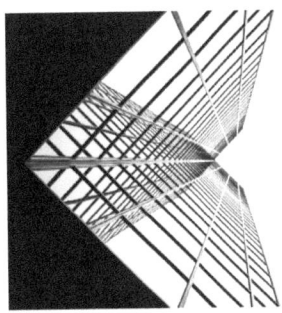 

Picture: 10.4 Group based on similarities becomes the Backdrop on noticing a movement

Neera said, "I will say something like this: Oh, one of those red windows suddenly opened!"

I said, "So, you will talk about *those red windows*. Won't you?"

Neera instantly understood that I had put emphasis on *those red windows*.

She said, "Wow, so the new backdrop is a collection of just the red windows! The windows are small and high up; yet I notice the red windows because they seemed pretty prominent in the otherwise grey picture with no noticeable highlight. And here I am, suddenly talking about one of the windows out of all the other red windows. The integrated sum of all the red windows is my new backdrop from which another movement is noticed!"

I said, "Let us see how a mind integrates multiple objects together." I then listed out a couple of ways in which the mind seemed to combine things into just a few meaningful things to notice at one time.

Proximity: *Things too close together are clubbed together*

In a random arrangement of objects, the mind groups the objects close together into one combined entity. The separate instruments played together give a composite sound of the orchestra. Individual spices and herbs added into a meal give out a comprehensive and unique flavor. The closely arranged little flowerets give an impression of a single flower; therefore are treated like a single flower by an observer.

Picture: 10.5 The proximity of little florets makes the assembly seen as a single flower. The mind sees three flowers

Features: *Things of the same features, such as size, shape or highlight are clubbed together*

In a random arrangement of objects, the objects of similar feature are seen as making one group even if they are not in proximity. We had already discussed in the past how all the red highlighted windows were seen together as a group of red windows. In a symphony, all the violin sounds are heard together, and so are all the drums played in synchronism. On a television screen little each group closely placed pixels of three basic colors (red, blue, green) appears to the mind as an individual pixel with a composite color made by a proportional combination of individual brightness of all three colors. For example, a flower shown on a television screen with only red and green pixels actually appears to be yellow.

In the following picture, all the colored candies get the attention out of the otherwise black and white background irrespective of their position in the field of observation.

Picture: 10.6 Things with similar features are seen as a collective group; all colored candies are seen as a group

The Outer: *The shape, pattern or sequence of the group defines the shape observed.*

When a number of objects are integrated into a bigger envelope of shape or a sequence, then the shape of individual objects being combined does not matter. This fact is also known as Gestalt psychology which explain this phenomenon as *"mind forms a global whole with self-organizing tendencies"*. In the picture below, the cluster of all squares is actually a sphere, a ball; and the cluster of all the spheres is actually a square.

Even though every element of the ball is made of square, it has the properties of a ball; it can roll even though none of its elements can roll. In the same way, even though each element of the square is a ball, it simply is a square; it cannot roll like a ball.

Picture: 10.7 The elements of a group do not represent the group. The group does not necessarily represent its elements (©2012-2017 Dracu-Teufel6666)

Neera asked me, "Papa, we have seen that the mind operates by differentiating as well as integrating. It differentiates changes to identify the movements out of the integrated constant background. How does becoming aware of this make on wiser?"

I said, "Knowing how the mind operates makes one wiser. When someone notices something, you know that the observation must have two components, the change or movement noticed and the background of noticing. The background is what one's conditioning is. In other words, a background (of observation) is what one is. What is noticed is nothing but the differentiation on the backdrop of one's conditioning."

Neera said, "I remember we had talked that the observer cannot see itself. We have now found out that the observer is nothing but the background of all the conditioning in terms of memory of past experiences and habits. Since one cannot see itself, the background cannot be seen because it itself is the seer; we call the background as empty, containing nothing. It is empty not because it is empty but because it cannot be seen. We had already said in the beginning that if something cannot be observed, it is not."

I said, "You have summarized it well. Since we have talked about it only intellectually, let's take some examples. What does it mean when we say that someone notices a circle?"

Neera asked, "What else can we mean besides the fact that someone is observing a circle?"

I asked back, "Who can notice a circle? What can we say about an observer who is observing a circle?"

Neera guessed, "Is the observer someone who has knowledge of what a circle is?"

I said, "Right. Only someone who has knowledge of what a circle is will notice a circle, if there is one. Anyone who has not known what a circle is will still notice a circle, but won't call it or name it a circle."

Neera said, "Ok. I can accept that. When I see something I have never known, I will still see its uniqueness, its color, its roughness or its shape, but I won't call it by what it is called, because I have no idea what it is called."

I asked her, "When someone calls you honest, what does it say about the observer?"

Neera said, "It means that the observer is the one who has some knowledge about what honesty is."

I added, "Or is not."

Neera said, "I didn't understand the is-not part. How is knowledge about the absence of something a conditioning in the background? I thought it could be only accumulation that makes up a background."

I said, "It's true that a background (of conditioning) is only accumulation; but it's an accumulation of knowledge and ideas. The observer in this case has an idea or knowledge about the word honesty. Once it knows what honesty is, it can observe if the honesty is present or absent in some movement, an observed entity."

> **A good conditioning is same as a bad conditioning in the sense that it is a conditioning, and it affects an observation.**

Neera said, "Oh, I get it! Knowledge is just a neutral entity. The accumulation in the mind does not care about presence or absence of it. A good conditioning is same as a bad conditioning in the sense that it is a conditioning, and it affects an observation."

I said, "You are right. If someone observes that you are honest, it shows that the observer has a conditioning which contains certain ideas about honesty. This person's idea of honesty might be totally different than another person's idea of honesty. When two different people observe you on a single quality, the honesty, the two might be in conflict based on their unique conditionings.

Neera said, "So basically, *you observe what you are!*"

I said, "Right! Do you think you are a bit wiser now?"

Neera said, "It is far more wisdom than I could expect. I can understand that when I read a news article, it is some fact presented by a writer, as an observer; an observer, who has a huge memory of cultural, social, political and religious experiences views all occurrences colored by one's own conditioning. An observer with strong religious background or someone interested in creating social disturbances will present news with elements of religious conflicts. All readers with their own conditioning will read such news and add their unique interpretations to color such articles with their own interpretation. In short, that which would have been just a quarrel between two people on an insignificant issue might become a spark for the communal fire in the society."

Neera added, "I am wiser now because when I read something, I will know that I need to filter out all positives and negatives in order to find out the raw knowledge."

I was glad that she was really becoming wiser. I wanted to make sure that she understood it as clearly as it sounded. I asked her to give me an example how she might filter something that she reads or views from some source.

Neera was glad to oblige. She thought for a moment. Then she said, "When someone mentions that a Muslim man was killed by a gang of Hindus, I will simply read it as a man killed by a group of people. I will not only remove the associations reported because they might be flawed, but I will also remove the concept of right and wrong, and simply see it as some happening where a person got killed. The only pure news I get out of this is that there were some people involved in an incident where someone got killed."

I was impressed, "That is such a sensible way of looking at things! Do you know when you are wise and observe everything in this way; you are stopping the damaging nature of conditioning in two ways?"

Neera asked, "In what two ways?"

I said, "First, you have made current observation without any past conditioning, so the observation was pure. Second, you have not created any additional conditioning, because there was nothing to store in the present moment. You notice only what is changing, and it is only relative movement that can be noticed. In absence of any discrimination, there was no new knowledge generated and so no new memory got created. You saw a happening and you observed it without memory or past experience. In essence an observation without conditioning in present moment also ensures that no future conditioning is created. Had you read this news as was reported without filtering the opposites, you would have read it partially or incompletely, based on your own conditioning of those opposites."

Neera said, "I know. If I were a Muslim I would have developed even more enmity towards Hindus. If I were a Hindu, I would have rationalized the whole incident as being justified in retaliation against some past incident. If I were from some other religion, I would still have looked at it as some enmity or closeness to one or the other party. It is only when the observation is made without conditioning that no more conditioning can be added to the observation."

I said to her, "Let me give you a few situations. Let's see if you can make a pure observation."

I spent some time thinking about different scenarios which one comes across during a day interacting with others at work, market, parties or at social network. I listed the situations and waited for Neera to interpret them without an observer, the conditioned entity.

1. A 3 year old child falls into a Gorilla enclosure at Cincinnati zoo. The zoo officials killed the Gorilla named Harambe. Thousands of people felt it was wrong to kill the Gorilla and hold the child's parents responsible for their carelessness.
2. A photo being shared on social media with a minister sitting in a conference hall with a flag of the country in front of him on the table being upside down.
3. A video being shared on social media where a girl is beating a boy on the road and everyone feels it was right.

Neera said, "Here is how I see these." Then she told me how she would have taken these messages.

1. There was a mishap at the zoo. A Gorilla was killed in order to save a child.
2. A flag is seen placed upside down on a table. A minister of the same country is seen sitting directly opposite to the improper flag in a conference.
3. The video shows a person being beaten by another.

I was impressed. I asked Neera how she was she able to filter the messages appropriately. She said, "You have already told me that the mind is born out of movements, and movements are nothing but the changes. A change or a contrast is made out of opposites, which is why it becomes known by the mind, like white on a black background, or a moving object on a stationary background. A conditioned observation is the one with extremes, the characteristics which have opposites. If I need to filter out the conditioning in an observation, I need to remove the opposites or any other tendencies of the mind such as taking existing knowledge as complete information. Any observation that involves memory and time is conditioned too."

I asked her to explain each example individually. She explained her reasoning like this.

1. In the moment of the crisis the zoo keepers made a decision. It was same as the 'scorpion' situation. The observation of crisis and the corresponding action are one comprehensive whole. The action by the zoo keepers was immediate, timeless and appropriate based on the observation. People's reaction is based on their observation which doesn't contain the same level of crisis as existed at the moment child was with the Gorilla. Any observation at a later moment is an observation in time, a conditioned observation with concepts such as right, wrong, duty, discipline etc.
2. A photo will always be deceiving in terms of sequence of events. I will recognize that the photo shows a flag being upside down beside a person who is possibly a

minister but it does not provide any more knowledge about the situation. The mind treats existing knowledge as complete, makes association and judges. The judgment could be wrong because the whole sequence of actions cannot be known from a snapshot. The association could be wrong, because a mistake on one part doesn't indicate mistake on all other parts too. Labelling, associating and using symbols comprise the nature of the mind, and I would rather avoid it.

3. I will see it as an act where a person is beating another. At no time will I have complete information. I will be aware that any information I will get about the incident might be greatly conditioned and incomplete. I will let go the mind's tendencies of dealing with extremes such as good versus bad, and identification such as woman being weak and men being naughty. I will also avoid the idea of who's right and justified for the act being done. I will just see the things as they are; a person being beaten by another person.

I learned something from Neera today. In order to be free of conditioning of human mind due to past experiences, we need not go to the beginning of time. At any moment, we need to be present to the facts as they are, devoid of the opposite extremes, which is nothing but our knowledge, because only *changes are known*. When facts are taken on their face value, we will not only see the things in their natural state, but we will also stop the mind from building any more content of conditioning that might affect future observations.

To overcome the mind, let go of opposites.

Neera asked me, "Please tell me more about the backdrop, or the background, which is the reference or ground of all observation."

I said, "I am glad that you asked, because there is still more to know about the nature of observed and observer. Let us look at the example of red windows again."

Neera said, "Sure."

I said, "We already saw that when your attention is on the red windows in the far side of the picture, you notice it when one or more or all of them suddenly opens."

Neera said, "This is right. In the picture it looks as if the red colored squares are window panes, the change in their color is noticed. This is the nature of the mind."

I said, "So a change of color in one or more of the windows out of all the red windows is noticed."

Neera said, "Yes. The noticing of the opening of one or more windows happens because of noticing of change in color against the new background created out of the integrated sum of all closed (red) windows."

"The feature noticed was a change in color. Was it a part of the background already?" I asked.

Neera agreed, "Yes, the change was noticed from the already known red color of the windows."

I asked, "Can we say that the red color of the pane was one of the attributes of the background? Was the change seen something that was already a part of the background, the observer?"

Neera said, "Yes, the change in red color was noticed because the background already contained the red color."

I asked, "Could you have noticed if one or more of the windows were made of plastic while some other were made of wood?"

Neera said, "No. The background got created out of an earlier movement, the integrated sum of all red colored windows. This integrated sum created from earlier noticing did not have any information about the content of windows."

I asked again, "Just like you noticed one or more of the windows suddenly opened, could you have noticed if one or more of the windows suddenly got wet with water?"

Neera said, "I don't think so, unless the color of those windows got changed due to their becoming wet. Otherwise, the information about window panes being dry or wet was not part of the earlier observation (out of the background created from all red windows)."

I asked once again, "Could you have known if one or more of those window panes suddenly got hot or cold?"

She said, "No. Our earlier observation was made on color distinction. A change of temperature cannot be noticed because the existing background got created only from earlier noticing of change in color, and not the temperature."

I said, "So you notice a sudden change in color of the windows just when you had been observing a set of all red colored windows in the background of the picture. But you could not have noticed a change in temperature or dryness or wetness of one or more. What does it say?"

Neera said, "The attention will always be on something which is already a part of the background, the observer. If the background does not contain a feature, no change in that feature can be observed on such background."

I said, "So the content of the new observation, attention or noticing is dependent on the content of the background."

Neera said, "Yes. The new is always out of the old."

I said, "Looking from the point of view of the background, it is the background which creates the new."

Neera said, "Yes. From the set of red windows, anything new will only be with reference to the color, never about other features which was never a part of the background."

I asked her, Can we apply the same logic to almost anything generally?"

Neera thought for a while, and then said, "I think we can. If I imagine a medical college with all doctors wearing white coats, we will notice any person without a white coat as not-a-doctor. The mind's attention to white coat forms a backdrop on which it notices the absence of white coat as a contrast. In a group of ducks quacking, any strange sound will be called as not-a-duck sound. The backdrop made out of the sound of ducks will be seen as a reference to notice any movement which has the same qualities as the backdrop itself."

I said, "Good Job! To summarize, we said that the background is the memory, the conditioning, the experiences collected since the birth till today. We also said that the background is the observer. You, the observer, the background, the collection of all your memories, experiences, habits, emotions and knowledge create the new observation based solely on what you are. In other words, you create your own world. The universe is born out of you!"

Neera was surprised. She had heard these kinds of statements many times. Many writers, motivators and spiritual leaders had mentioned such statements as you are the world, you create the world and you see what you are. She never thought they really meant anything. They looked like good statements, but they never made an impact. And here she was, pondering over the nature of observation with me for the past few weeks, and suddenly realizing that whatever is being observed has always been a part of her in some way.

This is why no person is ever able to understand other however hard one tries. No wonder the conflicts in the world are never going to end. What one tries to explain the other, cannot find way to the other's heart, because the other has had no experience of the things that is being asked for noticing.

The noticing cannot happen unless it already existed in the background. She understood everything. The source of the universe was nothing but her. She created a new world, entirely out of her experience or conditioning so far.

The noticing cannot happen unless it already existed in the background. She understood everything. The source of the universe was nothing but her. She created a new world, entirely out of her experience or conditioning so far. The observer was the observed. The observed was the observer. She knew who she was. She was nothing but her experiences, her habits. But what now? Will she remain like this; a prisoner of her experiences collected so far? Has she no hope to see things she has never known, seen or experienced? Does no one in the world have any hope of breaking the pattern, the condition of one's own mind? She was thinking. She was quiet. She was silent.

11

Nature of the Mind

Mind is fearful, insecure and a control freak

It was a Friday evening and Neera seemed quite excited. I asked her what she was up to. She told me that all the members of her NHS team were planning to go to some volunteer work on the next morning. In their school, they have formed a National Honors Society where students get a chance to take part in various leadership activities. Neera had told me that an exposure to social activities during the school time helped students get into good colleges. College admission committees not only looked at the scores, but also looked at the essays, extra-curricular activities, volunteer work and many leadership qualities in students.

I asked her, "What kind of leadership activity are you all planning?"

She said, "We have picked two streets along our school boundary which we will clean up by picking trash."

I asked her, "Is it not something that they have been doing every year?"

She said, "Yes, we discuss on many ideas but end up doing what was done in the past years."

I smiled and then said, "This is what the mind does. It doesn't want to enter into unknown. It will continue what it knows, because it is a safe territory."

"I want to know more about the Mind", Neera said.

"I know. This is the nature of the mind too." I replied.

Neera said, "I don't understand!"

I said, "Nature of the mind is to explore; to know more about the unknown. It is interested in stories."

Neera asked, "How is it interested in stories?"

I asked her back, "What do you think is a story?"

Neera said, "I know many stories; I have read plenty of them. But I don't know how to define what a story is."

I said, "If I were to define a story, I would say it is something that has a beginning, some description containing names and symbols and an end. Besides, it may have a purpose, but that doesn't seem totally necessary."

Neera seemed to think for a while. She asked, "But how can we say that the mind is always interested in stories?"

I said, "Let's find out. Just imagine a situation; a plain situation. For example, you and I are taking a walk in an unknown place."

Neera interrupted and asked, "Why an unknown place?"

I said, "Save the question for now. You will come to know why we started with an unknown place." Neera nodded.

I continued building the scenario and said, "So we go to an unknown place. We see a river. What do we do?"

Neera looked at me and asked, "What do we do?"

I said, "We could silently sit on the side of the river. We could put our legs in the water. We could watch the water flowing by. But there is certainly more. What would we do besides all these possibilities?"

Neera thought for a moment, and then said, "We could talk."

I asked, "And what could we talk?"

Neera said, "Since I have never been to this place and I come to this river, I might wonder what it is called. I might ask you if you knew where it came from or where did it go. I might also ask you if it flowed all year long or if there were any fishes in the river."

I said, "So we will be interested in the story; Right? There is no reason that we might sit there quietly, and later leave the place without wondering a bit about its origin, its destination and so many other questions jumping in our minds."

Neera said, "No way! We won't sit silently. We can't."

I said, "So, whatever happens, the mind will not just be with it silently observing the movements. Being silent is like death to the mind. Being without a story is like a death. And we know what it means to face death."

Neera said, "Yes, we said that a *movement is away from death*. Do you mean to say that the act of looking for a story is an escape from the death-like feeling in absence of a story in the present moment?"

I said, "Yes, the present moment is devoid of any past or future; meaning no beginning or end. Being silent without a story is like death, and the mind finds compulsion of a movement towards finding a story. A story containing the origin or the beginning and a destination or an end would give the solace to the otherwise dying mind. Mind loves stories. Mind IS a story; it exists in time. It has a beginning and an end."

Neera said, "It is an interesting way of looking at things."

I said, "Yes. The mind is a supreme entity. It always wishes to be in control of things around itself."

Neera asked, "How can we say that mind thinks of itself as the supreme entity or wishes control of things?"

I said, "It thinks of itself as supreme because there doesn't exist anything outside itself. Can you imagine anything that you have never seen, heard or known?"

Neera said, "No. My imagination is limited to what I have seen, heard, known or experienced so far, since my birth."

I asked, "Does this not mean that there is never anything beyond the mind? There cannot be. Mind is the supreme, and it knows it well."

Neera said, "I am still not convinced."

I said, "Let me give you an example. Do you feel bad when someone scolds or insults you?"

Neera said, "Yes, it is always uncomfortable and painful if someone is using insulting or abusive language."

I said, "Is it the pain that such verbal abuses cause? Or it is the lack of control that one has over the situation?"

Neera said, "I think it is the pain."

I said, "If you think that bad words cause pain, won't you feel pain every time someone uses abusive language?"

Neera said, "Yes, I think one would always feel pained at being abused, insulted or demeaned by someone."

I asked, "What if you are trying to make fun of someone; it could be his hair, or her accent? Would you feel hurt when the person gets mad, and starts abusing you when you are making fun of him or her?"

Neera said, "If I am making fun of someone and the other person gets mad or reacts with anger and abuses, it won't hurt me. I would be pleased of having instigated him; controlled him. The very fact that the person reacted shows me that I am in control. The other person is hurt because of losing the control of the situation."

I said, "The cause of pain is never because of the tone of voice, anger, language or any other violent behavior. It is always from the feeling of lack of control."

Neera said, "Yes, it makes sense."

I asked, "Do you know what you can do when you find yourself in a situation when you feel hurt and painful because of lack of control?"

Neera said, "If the situation is painful because of lack of control or because the control is in someone else's hands, I will have to either take control in my hands or let it go from the other person's hands."

I said, "That is right. But we don't usually do that. For example, when you try to make fun of other person's hair, the other person gives you control over him by reacting. What would happen when you try to make fun of someone's hair and the person doesn't seem to respond back?"

Neera said, "I will stop making fun after a couple of failed attempts. I would recognize that I have no control over the situation. I will not be interested in pursuing anymore."

I said, "Do you see, the mind is operating in exactly the same way whether it is the bully who is trying to make fun of other, or the other person who is being made fun of? It is all about control. When you lose control, you are not interested in doing it anymore. When he loses control, he feels pain. The mind is always trying to be in control; if not then the situation is either painful or not interesting to pursue."

Neera said, "This is really interesting. It is like an ever going game between the various copies of the mind working on the same basic rules."

I said, "That's right. The mind doesn't want to lose. Not being in control means losing. There is a very interesting example about this. Do you want to hear about it?"

Neera asked, "About controlling a situation which is out of control?"

I said, "Yes. It happened some time back when one of the young actresses appeared in a popular television program and could not reply when asked the name of the president."

Neera said, "I know. It was Alia Bhatt. People started making fun of her everywhere, especially on the social media. They started sharing jokes among each other and very soon the Alia jokes became synonymous with jokes highlighting her stupidity."

I asked Neera, "You mean to say that the name Alia became symbolic to idiocy!"

Neera said, "Right. As you had told me that the *mind loves symbols*. It made an association between the name Alia and stupidity."

I asked her, "Do you still see the jokes trending these days?"

Neera said, "No. They seemed to die suddenly. Nobody was sending any more Alia jokes."

I asked her, "Do you know how it might have happened?"

Neera said, "I have no idea."

I said, "It was actually Alia Bhatt herself who took the situation in her control. When she saw that she was being made fun of on every occasion about her stupidity, she thought of doing something unique. She came out with a video and shared it on social media. In this video she boasted of her own stupidity. When people saw that Alia was herself making fun of her own stupidity, it didn't interest them anymore to make fun of her. They had lost control over the situation."

Neera said, "I see! It is quite an intelligent step!"

I agreed with Neera. One who sees one's stupidity is intelligent. One who knows one's weaknesses is strong. It looks like a paradox but it isn't. Being intelligent or strong is not about having only positive or good qualities. It is about being able to remove the weaknesses. The constant knowledge of one's weaknesses will ensure that one is aware with present scenario. This will allow the appropriate actions based on the observation because *Observation is action* (Rule:10).

> **One who sees one's stupidity is intelligent. One who knows one's weaknesses is strong. It looks like a paradox but it isn't. Being intelligent or strong is not about having only positive or good qualities.**

Neera asked me, "When we say that the mind always wants to be in control, does it mean that the mind must be something fearful or insecure?"

I said, "You have made a right observation. Only someone who is weak, fearful or insecure will want to have a control. Mind is insecure by nature. It tries to hold on to the things it knows. It is afraid of the unknown."

Neera asked, "When we say that the mind is fearful or insecure, are we also saying that all the living creatures including humans are fearful and insecure too?"

I said, "Yes, the mind is the ground of all existence. Fear and insecurities are our deep rooted emotions. All we do is to be driven by our subtle fears. The way we live in societies, enforce norms and rules, adhere strongly to our beliefs and behave with each other on daily basis has its roots in our fears."

Neera said, "I don't understand this. I am not sure if I know what I fear."

I said, "We fear the unknown. We hold on to all that we know. We can say that the mind likes to be anchored to some fixed things or ideas."

"Such as?" Neera asked.

> "We fear unknown. We hold on to all that we know. We can say the mind likes to be anchored to some fixed things or ideas."

"Such as our habits, beliefs, possessions, knowledge and experience." I said.

Neera said, "Please explain this anchoring or attachment concept more. I don't really understand it."

I said, "Let's take a habit. It could be about something you eat or how you eat, something you wear or how you wear, a language you speak with a certain accent etc. What happens when someone points to your habit and tries to make you change it? If you are a vegetarian, how do you react when someone tries to make you eat meat? If you have never worn a skirt, how do you feel when you are asked to wear one on some occasion? What happens when someone points to you that you have a strange accent in your language?"

Neera said, "There is a strong resistance, an opposition whenever there is a threat to a habit."

I said, "Isn't it?"

Neera said, "Mind wants to hold on to it, the habit; the known."

I said, "This anchor, this attachment is the *home* for the mind. Do you know what home is?"

Neera asked, "In what sense?"

I said, "A home is the ground, the base, where the mind is completely relaxed and at peace. No matter how far the mind wants to go and how tired it becomes, a home is what the mind will always retire to. A sleep is like a home too, to the mind. After a daylong tiresome action, the mind gets its complete relaxation by coming to home, to sleep."

Neera nodded. She was listening.

I said, "All our habits, possessions, knowledge and beliefs are the anchors which are like a home to the mind. Being fearful and insecure, it is always attached to its anchors, holding on to them tightly. Taking the attachments away from the mind is painful. *A mind resists pain.* It resists getting away from its anchor. Have you seen a child holding on tightly to its dad? If you offer a toy or a chocolate to the child, it will extend its hands to grab it, but won't loosen its hold on its dad. If it senses that the toy or the chocolate is far enough for it to let go of the hold of its dad, it won't try anymore to get its reward; not at the cost of losing its anchor. A child is simply a pure mind in action; not corrupted by habits, conditioning or knowledge."

Neera was listening quietly.

I continued, "Do we ever want to lose what we possess? What happens when we lose something? Don't we feel pain? What happens when the government announces increase in taxes? Doesn't an increase in tax mean that everyone has to lose a part of what was in their possession? Is there any single person who is not uncomfortable with the idea of increased taxes? What happens when the company announces a bonus to its employees? Is there a single person who doesn't want to get more of what one is attached to?"

Neera said, "It is so surprising. I remember our very first discussion when we questioned whether humans were the most intelligent species in the universe. It seems we are simply some automated script being operated by standard algorithm with some basic rules!"

"The algorithm called the Mind." I said.

Neera said, "I can understand clearly that it is the mind which holds on to the things that it feels at home with. And we humans should possess the ability to use our intellect greatly beyond the subtle tendencies of the mind. But why do we need to go away from what the mind wants to do? What's wrong in continuing the same way as we and everybody has been going on?"

I said, "We will have to understand what it means to hold on to some fixed ground, an anchor. We will have to understand what an attachment clearly means. We will also have to know if it is a wise to be afraid to let go of the known and dive into the unknown."

Neera said, "I would definitely want to know, if there is anything wrong with holding on to fixed ideas and possessions."

I asked, "What does it mean when you say you don't want to let go? Is it not the same thing as saying you are afraid of the change; afraid to change?"

Neera said, "Sure, being attached to something and not letting go is exactly a way of saying one doesn't want change."

I asked, "What did we say a change is? What did we say a non-changing thing is?"

Neera said, "We said that observer is something non-changing, a fixed frame of reference. We also found out that what is changing is what is observed."

I asked her again, "And what is an appropriate action that will always have unlimited potential in human beings or any living being for that matter? What is an action that will be limited, exhaustive and incomplete?"

Neera said, "We said that a pure observation leads to a total action. A total action is boundless, full of energy. A conditioned observation is always limited and exhaustive."

I said, "Being afraid of change, continuing to stick to fixed, permanent and non-changing, we continue to live unaware of the changing surroundings. We continue to act in limited and incomplete ways. This is all due to the deep rooted tendencies of the mind to hold on to some fixed attributes, such as ideas, habits and knowledge. Do you think it is intelligent to live on the will of the mind?

Neera said, "Definitely not. On the contrary the mind can be made to be observant of the subtle changes happening around it. It is not wise to remain dull and unobservant just because the mind feels safe in remaining the way it is, grounded in its being."

I said, "Shouldn't the mind be trained to drop attachments?

Neera asked, "How can we drop attachment, the anchor?"

I asked her back, "Do you know what it means to drop the attachments?"

Neera said, "I am not sure; but it seems that in holding on to our attachment to the known, we are continuing to feed our fears."

I said, "Letting go of the anchor means losing ground. When a ship lets go of the anchor, it is free to roam in the vast ocean; the whole unknown territory. Unknown is like a death. The mind is afraid to die. By asking how to get rid of anchor you are asking how the mind can be asked to die."

Neera said, "I suppose. This looks like a deadlock. If you hold on to your attachment, you live fearfully. If you let go, you face death."

I said, "Death is simply unknown. A mind is afraid of the unknown. There is no deadlock. You know that in attachments there is a fear; but you don't know anything in non-attachment. You simply fear because you don't know. Maybe there was nothing dangerous in non-attachment. Maybe it was just an imagination of the mind. Maybe by letting go, the mind experiences total freedom, a freedom which the bound and conditioned mind could not even imagine."

> **This looks like a deadlock. If you hold on to your attachment, you live fearfully. If you let go, you face death.**

Neera was silent. There was no deadlock. There was a known which was scary and then, there was an unknown. When something is unknown, then nothing can be said about it. The only option is to jump in the unknown and get to experience it. The mind has to face its death. The mind has to turn its direction. It must die.

She asked me, "Some religions tell you to practice non-attachment. Is it not one way to go about it?"

I asked, "Don't you see the paradox!"

Neera asked, "A paradox; where?"

I said, "To practice is to create a habit. We said a habit, an attachment or a holding on is the same thing. Non-attachment is when you don't practice, don't create a habit. In Jainism, the followers practice non-attachment by taking a vow to drop a habit, such as not to eat a particular kind of food; onion or potato, for example."

Neera was silent. There was no deadlock. There was a known which was scary and then, there was an unknown. When something is unknown, then nothing can be said about it.

Neera asked, "Are you trying to imply that someone practicing non-attachment by refraining from a particular habit is not helping in any way?"

I said, "What is non-attachment? If you like something a lot, then you are attached. If you dislike something a lot, then you are attached too; you are attached to the dislike, the hate. Ideally, when you let go your attachment, you let go everything, every emotion, every feeling, every thought about the thing. A true non-attachment is having no particular liking for a potato or an onion, for example. If you happen to find potato in your food, you eat. If you happen to find it missing in something which should have a potato, you simply eat. You don't complain. That is non-attachment. Non-attachment is an I-don't-care attitude. If the potato cannot make you feel uncomfortable in any way, then you are truly non-attached to a potato."

I saw Neera was quietly trying to understand this. She had seen some of her friends who had taken a vow not to eat onion and potato in their food. They strongly believed that the practice of selective non-attachment to some objects put them in a better control of their lives. What she had seen and heard in life so far seemed to be falling apart.

I thought I could explore this aspect in depth with her. I asked Neera, "What do you think an object is."

Neera said, "I don't know what you are asking. An object is just a thing. I won't be able to describe what a thing is; but maybe it is something that can be seen, heard, or perceived?"

I said, "Let's look at the whole thing in a different way. If you call something a rose, or an apple, what is it that is a rose or an apple?"

Neera said, "A rose can be something that looks like a rose, smells like a rose, feels the touch of a rose. Same is true for an apple, which can be something that looks, smells and tastes like an apple."

I asked, "Can you call something an apple if it doesn't taste like an apple? Though, it may look and smell like an apple."

Neera said, "No. If it doesn't taste like an apple, it is not an apple. The looks and smell would not make any object an apple."

I asked, "Can you call something an apple if it doesn't look like an apple? Though it may smell and taste like an apple."

Neera said, "No. If it doesn't look like an apple, it is not an apple. The smell and taste of an apple doesn't make something an apple."

I said, "So, an object or a thing is nothing but its characteristics; *all of its characteristics.*"

Neera said, "This doesn't look right. You mean the truth is not in object but just in its characteristics?"

I asked, "Is it not so? When you bring fresh tomatoes from the market, how do you know they are fresh tomatoes?"

Neera said, "Because they look, smell, and feel like fresh tomatoes. We can see their bright red color and texture of their skin."

I said, "You see the red color and tight textured tomatoes and you think that they are fresh tomatoes. But nowhere in your observation you can know if the red color was mischievously injected by someone in the raw and green tomatoes to give them that look."

Neera got silent. It was true. *If something is not observed, it doesn't exist.* One doesn't see or know about someone manipulating with the fruits and vegetables, so one sees and knows the vegetables to be fresh and pure. There is no way to know an object except by the way of perceiving through eyes, ears, nose, tongue, or touch. What the senses tell us is the truth for us. *No knowledge can ever be complete.* No truth can ever be total. There is always something not gathered by the senses, therefore, not known. *What is not known doesn't exist*; because if it did, then no one could ever be cheated, fooled or taken advantage of. A person doesn't get cheated intentionally. Everybody gets cheated because they get the truth or reality wrong or incomplete; their perception

What the senses tell us is the truth for us. No knowledge can ever be complete. No truth can ever be total. There is always something not gathered by the senses, therefore, not known.

gives them a different picture of the reality; a picture different than what it truly is.

RULE 18: Objects or things are nothing but their characteristics.

I said to Neera, "We are saying that an object is nothing but its characteristics. A potato is something that looks like a potato, smells like a potato and tastes like a potato. It is same as saying that anything that looks like a potato, smells like a potato and tastes like a potato IS a potato!"

Neera said, "That seems quite right."

I said, "Some religious people who decide not to eat potato replace every potato based food preparation with raw banana. Do you think they really got rid of potato? A raw banana looks like a potato and tastes like a potato in a cooked food and therefore, is a potato. Those who practice non-attachment to potato continue to relish all such special dishes which are known to contain potatoes. A practice of not eating potato while continuing to replace every potato based food with a raw banana is exactly what is not a non-attachment."

Neera said, "So it means that a non-attachment does not mean detachment. Does it mean neither attachment, nor detachment?"

I said, "Right. *Being free of opposites is the non-attachment.* When the mind is free of the opposites, it becomes free.

There is nothing to hold on. You lose your home when you are free."

Neera asked, "Why must losing your home only make you free? Can you not be at home and still free?"

I said, "Being at home means being with the frame of reference (of observation). A home means familiarity; there is nothing unknown, nothing unsure, nothing scary. A home is all your habits, conditionings, culture, likes, dislikes, desires and dreams. Being at home you are comfortable but susceptible to all kinds of misinformed observations."

Neera said, "Why are our observations misinformed when we are at home?"

I replied, "Because the observation is conditioned. Remember, we already talked about it."

Neera said, "Oh, right. I thought being at home was the most desirable thing for a sane person."

I said, "It can be the most desirable thing for someone, if the home was devoid of everything; no desires, memory, habits or expectations."

Neera said, "Please explain me once again how being at home our observations won't be pure and unconditioned."

I said, "Being at home means being with the things familiar to you, like your habits. Imagine that you prefer a cooler temperature. You are comfortable at any place where temperatures are generally low. If someone asks you to compare two cities, your comparison will be highly influenced by your own comfort levels if those cities have very different temperatures. Your comparison will be biased by your own choices. If you were to suggest to a friend a better place to visit out of the two, you will prefer the place which is cooler. Being free of attachments is being free totally."

What started with a discussion on the movement came to end on the nature of the mind. The mind is a movement; a movement in time. The universe too is a movement. The universe as observed by the mind is always incomplete, always suffering, because the observation is always limited. Only changes are noticed and as long as things don't change, there is no observation. The end of the mind is the only way out. The mind, born out of the time, must die. It will die, if the time stops. The time must stop.

12

Wrapping it all

What decides what action happens on noticing a movement.

Neera asked me, "I remember you compared the activity of the mind with a child many times during our discussion. You said that the mind tries to hold on to some fixed anchor like a child holds on tightly to its dad even when trying to grab something with other hand. You also characterized the mind as a lazy entity, trying to make things easier for it all the time. You gave many examples of how almost everybody in this world is unknowingly behaving what the mind is programmed to do. You had mentioned that the observation pairs up with an appropriate action to form a unified whole. I am not sure how a child, a lazy person, a normal person or a wise person acts following an observation (of movement). I would like to know how an appropriate action gets decided for each of them."

I said, "We have known the qualities of the mind. We have known that the mind is lazy, controlling, pattern seeking, habit forming and memorizing entity. We also know that in most of the situations, the actions taken by the mind are not the most intelligent decisions. On the contrary, most of the actions taken even by the most powerful, educated, and smart people are totally mechanical choices, taken simply from the level of the mind. Depending on the past performance, impressive resumes and referrals for evaluating a person while hiring for a job are such actions that almost everyone takes without knowing that it's a trap of the mind. People unequivocally getting impressed by outgoing and extrovert people everywhere and awarding them favors prove that they let the mind take the most sophisticated decisions. They have no clue that all they know is what has been known through senses. What is not seen or heard by them doesn't exist in their awareness. Let me explain you how the mind works in each one out of a child, a lazy, a normal and a wise person."

Neera became comfortable in her couch, well aware that I was going to draw some flow-chart. She was right. We were going to formulate an idea which was not familiar to most people. The knowledge had always been there, but had not been easily explained or understood by most. We tried to understand the basics of observation, action and the nature of the mind to arrive at the process which takes place with every movement differently from the reference of a child, a lazy person, a normal person and a wise one.

I said, "Let's start investigating. Assume that there is a movement which is noticed. What happens at the very moment the movement is noticed?"

Neera said, "The moment a movement is noticed, the memory storage is checked if it is something already known or not."

I said, "Good. What happens when the memory is checked?"

Neera said, "When the memory is checked, there could be two alternatives. Either the movement is similar to something already known or it is something entirely new."

We two had already gone over all these aspects in our previous investigations over the past few weeks. Neera didn't find any trouble in coming up with the facts. She had pretty much understood that the mind could either be conditioned with previous memories or could be totally fresh if there was no past remembrance. I asked her again, "If the mind has sufficient knowledge about the movement, what does it do?"

Neera thought silently for a while. Then she continued thinking loudly, "If the mind knows a movement already, then it must also know the corresponding action because the remembrance must be of the previous movement as well as past actions and all the associated activities. If the mind knows everything, then being lazy and easy going, it need not do anything new which could otherwise complicate the things unnecessarily."

I interrupted her loud thinking and said, "So, we understand it well that as long as there is sufficient knowledge of the movement, the mind continues to be in its comfort zone. It continues to carry out all the actions as it has been doing in the past which has a known pattern and a predictable outcome."

I asked Neera, "Should we draw a flow diagram for the mind in comfort zone?"

Neera nodded. I picked up a pencil and drew the simple picture representing the lazy mind enjoying its comfort zone.

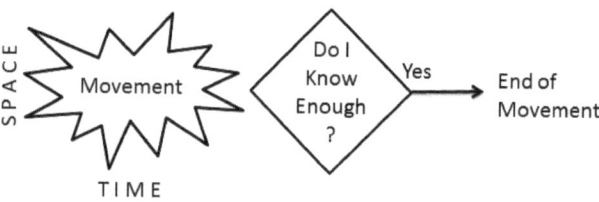

Picture: 12.1 Observation and Movement in a comfort zone

I asked Neera, "Do you want to explore some practical situations which fall under the comfort zone for the mind?"

Neera said, "Sure. You give me an idea which will help me gather some examples."

I said, "What about a situation such as watching movies of your favorite actors?"

Neera said, "It sure is the comfort zone. I know enough about my actors, their strengths, weaknesses and I love to get more of the same experiences that they have given me in past. If I am made to watch a movie where I don't know the actors, then I have to find some real reason to continue watching the movie, like a good plot or some thrilling experience. It would be very uncomfortable to go out of my comfort zone to watch any random movie with random stars. Let me think another example now. What about spending your time the way you normally do? For example, I like to take a walk in the backyard every evening after dinner. This is something I don't want to miss."

I said, "Good one. So, that is your comfort zone. When you are taken out of this schedule, you will miss it terribly. In the similar way a comfort zone is also in continuing all your habits such as drinking tea or coffee, smoking or not smoking, reading or avoiding reading, playing or avoiding playing, socializing with friends and relatives etc."

Neera said, "That covers up almost all of our activities in a normal day! Doesn't it mean that having opinions about various things in our own ways, carrying our prejudices, beliefs, faiths and experiences and being proud of them could also be our comfort zone?"

I said, "True. Everything that we are and we do is our comfort zone. Our knowledge is basically our comfort zone. Our knowledge is our biggest hurdle in getting to know the world better!"

Neera said, "A normal family life, a routine life such as that of a housewife or a government employee or a factory worker doing repeated job are all simply the activities of a lazy mind! This is kind of scary!"

I said, "Yes, it is a scary thought to find out that the knowledge (past experiences) itself paralyzes further knowledge. Almost every person spends most time of the day performing routine activities totally unaware and unmindful. The mind has sufficient memory of the past to carry out the necessary actions."

Our knowledge is basically our comfort zone. Our knowledge is our biggest hurdle in getting to know the world better!

It was about time to summarize the rest of the alternatives to the question, "Do I know enough?" The answer to this question results in creation of the rest of human universe, our world. It is the world of opposites, the world created by our conditioned mind, the world which is nothing but an eternal sleep of the smartest creation of this universe, the humans. It is the zone of the *Knowable*. It is the obvious choice of the mind where it can either know more about the movement or it cannot know about it. Whatever the choice, the mind gets busy continuously influenced by the operation of opposing forces; of pleasure and pain. Once born such, the movement of mind can either stop at certain time or can continue to run endlessly, through eternity.

For example, a person is given a difficult task at his office. The job at office is the 'knowable' zone where he either knows how to do it or he doesn't know it. If he knows how to do it, he is engaged in a tiring schedule of carrying it out in best possible way for the expectation of reward. If he doesn't know how to do it, he is engaged in a tiring schedule of trying to find out what can be done living in fear of possible punishment, if he is unable to do the job. The field of 'knowable' is the one in which all the rest of the working people are trapped, the endless zone of tiring and stressful action. The Buddha called it 'samsara', the field of rewards and punishments.

Once I was asked to back up my brother's car. It had a manual drive and I attempted to move the car with my existing twenty years old memory of using manual gears. I saw the picture on the gear stick and tried to put the car in 'reverse', but was unsuccessful. Every time it landed on first gear. I continued to try several time but was unable to make it go reverse. I stopped, tried to think creative or out of the box, but could not come up with any other way except for trying even harder on the gear handle. I was operating in the zone where I knew that there was a way and I didn't know exact way to operate. I had to finally call my brother to tell me what was different in that car that I could not figure out.

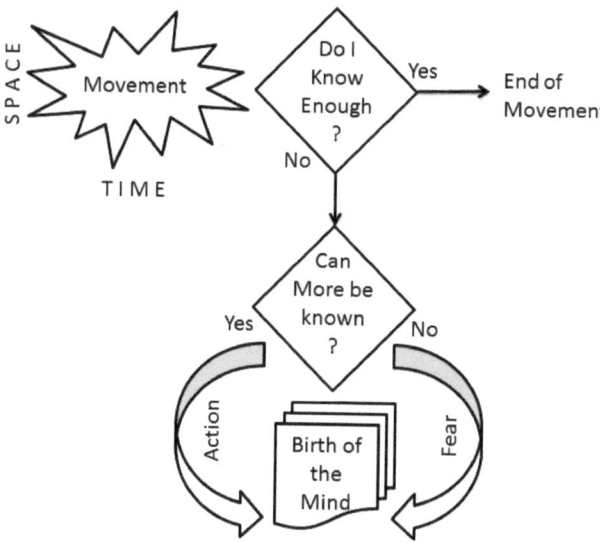

Picture 12.2: Observation and Movement in the zone of the Known

Neera asked, "How does a child act on noticing a movement?"

I said, "He simply acts."

"And a wise one?" Neera asked.

"*I don't know.*" I said.

Neera gave a smile.

Appendix – A

Ground Rules

1. Movement happens in time
2. To Observe is to Know
3. Frame of Reference (of a movement) is the point of observation, or simply is the observer
4. Frame of Reference or observer is non-moving
5. Observer cannot see itself
6. Only change is noticed
7. Attention is movement
8. There is no observation in absence of movement
9. There is no movement in absence of an observer
10. Observation is Action
11. All movement is away from death
12. Pain is death
13. All movement is away from pain
14. All effort is towards avoiding death in the present moment
15. The (idea of) death doesn't matter if it's not in the present moment
16. There is no difference between a thing and an idea of the thing for the mind
17. Symbols mean more than the things or ideas they symbolize
18. Objects or things are nothing but their characteristics

Index

attention, 40, 41, 42, 43, 263

awareness, 41, 256

fear, 110, 181, 201, 242, 247, 261

intelligence, 9, 110

intelligent, 2, 92, 110, 134, 153, 172, 176, 179, 194, 195, 240, 241, 244, 246, 256

knowledge, 8, 9, 29, 32, 33, 35, 36, 37, 38, 51, 56, 57, 58, 91, 110, 140, 143, 148, 150, 151, 152, 154, 166, 177, 180, 196, 205, 207, 208, 209, 210, 211, 212, 213, 220, 221, 222, 223, 230, 241, 242, 243, 246, 251, 256, 257, 258, 260

meditation, 13, 48

memory, 108

movement, 1, 2, 3, 4, 5, 6, 7, 8, 9, 11, 12, 14, 15, 16, 17, 18, 20, 21, 22, 23, 26, 28, 30, 31, 32, 39, 40, 41, 42, 43, 44, 45, 46, 51, 53, 54, 55, 56, 57, 58, 59, 63, 70, 71, 73, 74, 76, 77, 79, 80, 81, 83, 85, 86, 87, 90, 91, 97, 103, 104, 109, 110, 111, 112, 115, 116, 122, 123, 124, 126, 127, 129, 131, 136, 137, 139, 140, 142, 143, 144, 145, 147, 148, 149, 150, 151, 155, 157, 158, 159, 162, 175, 177, 181, 186, 187, 188, 189, 194, 196, 207, 209, 210, 211, 213, 215, 219, 221, 223, 228, 229, 236, 255, 256, 257, 258, 260, 262, 263

observation, 15, 18, 19, 20, 21, 22, 23, 24, 28, 29, 30, 32, 35, 36, 37, 39, 40, 43, 44, 45, 46, 47, 48, 53, 56, 58, 61, 70, 71, 73, 77, 79, 80, 81, 83, 84, 85, 86, 87, 90, 91, 92, 95, 96, 97, 98, 99, 100, 101, 104, 109, 110, 111, 115, 116, 117, 118, 120, 122, 123, 126, 130, 131, 132, 135, 136, 137, 138, 139, 140, 142, 143, 144, 145, 146, 148,

150, 151, 152, 157, 162, 166, 177, 179, 184, 196, 205, 207, 208, 209, 210, 211, 212, 217, 219, 221, 223, 224, 225, 227, 228, 229, 230, 231, 241, 246, 251, 253, 255, 256, 263
observer, 15, 20, 21, 22, 23, 24, 35, 36, 45, 53, 59, 63, 85, 99, 100, 140, 142, 143, 144, 145, 146, 148, 152, 208, 209, 211, 216, 219, 220, 221, 222, 224, 227, 228, 229, 230, 231, 245, 263
paradox, 182, 241, 247, 248
pattern, 98, 144, 175, 176, 184, 185, 186, 187, 188, 189, 190, 191, 192, 193, 194, 195, 196, 197, 199, 202, 218, 231, 256, 258
symbol, 30, 185, 194, 195, 196, 197, 198, 200, 201, 203, 205, 212
truth, 33, 39, 47, 48, 49, 52, 53, 61, 64, 65, 66, 67, 68, 69, 70, 71, 72, 73, 74, 75, 76, 79, 172, 198, 203, 250, 251
universe, 2, 4, 5, 8, 9, 12, 14, 38, 46, 47, 63, 74, 82, 85, 86, 90, 95, 99, 100, 101, 110, 111, 112, 113, 122, 129, 135, 136, 141, 150, 151, 156, 159, 161, 162, 165, 177, 178, 188, 209, 230, 231, 244, 260

www.ingramcontent.com/pod-product-compliance
Lightning Source LLC
Chambersburg PA
CBHW042055290426
44111CB00001B/12